Learning for Uncert

Learning for Uncertainty explores technology's role in education, specifically unpacking the question: How should educators prepare today's children for a world that has yet to be made?

As technology evolves faster than our capacity to fully understand the social, cultural, economic, and moral implications of many innovations, today's educators are tasked with the unique role of preparing students to capitalize on technology's opportunities and also mitigate its dangers to their society, to democratic processes, and to institutions. Veteran educators McDiarmid and Zhao explore the implications of emerging technologies for future jobs, organizations, students, and learning, covering topics such as

- The future of work and workers as technology eliminates some industries while creating new ones.
- Potential futures, both bright and dark, awaiting students.
- The qualities, dispositions, social behaviors, and skills that are likely to advantage students in the future.
- The possibility of technology to revolutionize education in ways that will better position students for an uncertain future.
- How technology can free teachers from time and effort devoted to routine matters to instead assume roles that are potentially more satisfying and supportive of their students' learning.
- Learning opportunities and educator roles that have the potential to bring about needed changes.
- Capitalizing on these uncertain times to rethink curriculum, pedagogy, opportunities to learn, and the organization of school as well as the roles of students, educators, parents, and policymakers.

This latest book in the *Routledge Leading Change* series is ideal reading for educators and policymakers in both P–12 and higher education interested in ensuring our education systems provide the experiences and learning opportunities necessary to cultivate the innovative, iconoclastic, and generative thinkers and creators needed for a future that nourishes the minds, bodies, and spirits of all.

G. Williamson McDiarmid is the former Dean and Alumni Distinguished Professor *Emeritus* at the University of North Carolina, Chapel Hill, North Carolina, and Distinguished Chair of Education at East China Normal University, Shanghai, China.

Yong Zhao is Foundation Distinguished Professor of Education at the University of Kansas, Kansas, and Professor of Educational Leadership at the Melbourne Graduate School of Education, Australia.

8-3-2022

Routledge Leading Change Series

Series Editors: Andy Hargreaves & Pak Tee Ng

The world is crying out loud for quality education, and for the type of leadership and change to make quality education a reality. Never has there been a greater need for grasping the big pictures of leadership and change in education, which creates the world of tomorrow by developing future generations today. This is especially pertinent as we contemplate the disruptions caused by COVID-19 and the education landscape in a post-pandemic world.

In this series, you will find some of the world's leading intellectual authorities on educational leadership and change. From the pens of writers such as Dennis Shirley, Pak Tee Ng, Andy Hargreaves, Michael Fullan, Amanda Datnow, Vicky Park, Santiago Rincón-Gallardo, Armand Doucet, Yong Zhao, and Bill McDiarmid, come wise insights and breakthrough ideas on this subject. They ask what the new imperatives of educational change are. They explore the paradoxical nature of educational change in celebrated Asian cultures and systems like those of Singapore. They point to the power of professional collaboration and leading from the middle in schools, and networks of schools and across the world, rather than just driving change from the top. They invite us to think about and pursue educational change as social movements aimed at liberating learning. They highlight the surreal nature of leadership and change at this critical moment in world history.

This series of books is for the stout-hearted and open-minded reader who is keenly looking for inspiration to unlock the potential of educational leadership and change in this turbulent world.

Published books in the series include:

Learning from Singapore: The Power of Paradoxes
By Pak Tee Ng

Surreal Change: The Real Life of Transforming Public Education
By Michael Fullan

Professional Collaboration with Purpose: Teacher Learning Towards Equitable and Excellent Schools
By Amanda Datnow and Vicki Park

Liberating Learning: Educational Change as Social Movement
By Santiago Rincón-Gallardo

Teaching Life: Our Calling, Our Choices, Our Challenges
By Armand Doucet

Learning for Uncertainty: Teaching Students How to Thrive in a Rapidly Evolving World
By G. Williamson McDiarmid and Yong Zhao

For more information about this series, please visit: https://www.routledge.com/Routledge-Leading-Change-Series/book-series/RLCS.

Learning for Uncertainty

Teaching Students How to Thrive in a Rapidly Evolving World

G. Williamson McDiarmid and Yong Zhao

NEW YORK AND LONDON

Cover image: Getty Images

First published 2022
by Routledge
605 Third Avenue, New York, NY 10158

and by Routledge
2 Park Square, Milton Park, Abingdon, Oxon, OX14 4RN

Routledge is an imprint of the Taylor & Francis Group, an informa business

Library of Congress Cataloging-in-Publication Data
Names: McDiarmid, G. Williamson, author. | Zhao, Yong, 1965-author.
Title: Learning for uncertainty: teaching students in a rapidly evolving world/ G. Williamson McDiarmid, Yong Zhao.
Description: New York, NY: Routledge, 2022. |
Series: Routledge leading change series |
Includes bibliographical references and index.
Identifiers: LCCN 2021037255 (print) | LCCN 2021037256 (ebook) |
ISBN 9781138926967 (hardback) | ISBN 9781138926974 (paperback) |
ISBN 9781315682884 (ebook)
Subjects: LCSH: Education–Effect of technological innovations on. |
Education–Aims and objectives.
Classification: LCC LB1028.3 .M3926 2022 (print) | LCC LB1028.3
(ebook) | DDC 370.11–dc23
LC record available at https://lccn.loc.gov/2021037255
LC ebook record available at https://lccn.loc.gov/2021037256

ISBN: 978-1-138-92696-7 (hbk)
ISBN: 978-1-138-92697-4 (pbk)
ISBN: 978-1-315-68288-4 (ebk)

DOI: 10.4324/9781315682884

Typeset in Adobe Caslon Pro
by Deanta Global Publishing Services, Chennai, India

Dedicated to our children and students

Contents

Introduction

The Context

How do we prepare our children for a world that is yet to be made? This is the question we want to address, and we try to explore in this book.

As we write this, educators across the globe are struggling to educate students amid a worldwide pandemic. Many are being stretched to adopt and use unfamiliar instructional technologies and pedagogies. For their part, most students, who might be quite comfortable with social media, are trying to adapt to unfamiliar ways of interacting and learning, with mixed success. As stressful as the situation is for educators, students, and their families, the adoption of online teaching and learning technologies is accelerating changes that were likely inevitable. Even prior to the pandemic, online education was on the rise and some teachers had begun to use various new technologies such as Zoom, class management systems, and flipped classrooms.

Looking into the near and mid-future, this generation's facility and comfort with various technologies are essential. They will face a world of work increasingly shaped by technology. Many current jobs will fade away or be significantly altered by technology. Many new jobs will be created by evolving technologies that we cannot foresee.

DOI: 10.4324/9781315682884-1

Technology is already changing daily life, from smart homes to driverless cars to wearable tech. Not only is change occurring but it is occurring at an increasingly rapid pace.

The pandemic has also spurred the rapid evolution and adoption of technologies that improve and save lives. Telemedicine expanding dramatically in 2020 and 2021. Unable to see patients face to face, medical professionals are diagnosing and treating illnesses with the help of a range of technologies, crowdsourcing, and "big data." Recent discoveries about DNA and RNA as well as clustered regularly interspaced short palindromic repeats (CRISPR) technology enable cell-level manipulations of genes. A greater understanding of RNA informed the development of vaccines that are effective in shielding us from the Covid-19 virus.

Returning to the issue of social media, we are also writing at a time when social media is under greater scrutiny than ever before. The rise and proliferation of social media have enabled people everywhere to connect and communicate and share joys, sorrows, grievances, laughter, cat antics, baby's first step, and more. Online communities such as those for programmers enable developers to learn from others' discoveries and mistakes. The darker side of online communities was exposed by the attack on the US Capitol on January 6, 2021. The insurrectionists planned and coordinated their attack via several social media platforms. Social media has opened Pandora's box of outrage, hatred, misinformation, and conspiracies that have led, as we have recently witnessed, to violence.

Awareness of and concerns about the increasing power of "big tech" – Amazon, Apple, Alphabet, Facebook, Microsoft – are also growing. As they accumulate data about us, their power continues to grow. A 2018 Pew survey found that 95% of teens have access to smartphones and 45% report being online almost constantly (Anderson & Jiang, 2018). Recording, saving, and aggregating every keystroke and applying proprietary algorithms to the amassed data, these largely unaccountable private companies may know more about us than our family and friends. Their goal is to monetize the resulting volume of data they collect, a goal that research on human behavior has significantly aided and abetted. As a recent documentary on social media demonstrated, what big tech wants most is for us to return again and again, almost like Skinner's pigeons returning repeatedly to feed – in the case of humans, to feed our psychological needs. Each time we return to a page or a website, we are providing more information about ourselves: our wants, needs, fears, insecurities, obsessions. Online retailers as well as political operatives pay large sums for these data and apply their own algorithms that enable them to manipulate our emotions, vulnerabilities, and even self-image.

This is not, of course, the whole story about new technologies. Technology has created a different world and made the world both worse and better for everyone. Technology is inextricably intertwined with geopolitical events and the shifting order in the world. While the term "globalization" is perhaps relatively new, the phenomenon is not. Global trade has been going on for centuries, even before the Silk Road and the Incense Trade Route of lore. The world had been steadily growing with occasional and temporary declines such as the current pandemic-related downturn.

The world has, indeed, become a global village, but a village consisting of many different tribes, some of whom have benefited disproportionately from globalization. The potential for major conflicts within nations and among nations remains great. Competition for scarce resources, land, and markets is probably as fierce as ever – as are nationalism and collective national grievances. The future of geopolitics is filled with uncertainty and unknowns as technologies continue to accelerate globalization as well as the potential of nations to use technology to spy on and disrupt rivals.

Technology and the economy are deeply intertwined. The widening opportunity and income gaps are partially responsible for today's political and social unrests globally and will doubtlessly continue until addressed properly. As in the past, the future world economy will likely see major upturns and downturns, but how inequality among different groups within a nation and among groups across nations is addressed will significantly shape the future. Climate change likely will continue to exacerbate inequities as a warming world will force population migrations from parched lands to seek lives in more temperate climates. According to the *New York Times*, although 1% of the world is currently a "barely livable hot zone," by 2070, 19% of the earth will be so (Lustgarten, 2020). Among future uncertainties is: Where will the people in the hot zones go?

The Challenge for Education

So what does all this have to do with schools and schooling? Everything. A primary role of schools is to prepare students to live in the future. The future is not prefabricated, just waiting for the arrival of today's students. Rather, the future is what today's and future graduates will create. Even as we write, students are shaping the world as they mature, although their contribution is relatively modest compared to the impact they will have on the future.

To say that technologies are mere tools is true – even if it is also a truism. This is, however, the starting claim for the contention that to productively wield technology requires humans who understand both technology and themselves, possess the knowledge to capitalize on technology's affordances and mitigate its dangers, and the moral judgment to determine when it is and isn't being employed for the betterment of their communities and society.

Our Questions

The questions for us are: Are we preparing students to both take advantage of what emerging technologies offer and recognize the potential dangers that these technologies – especially social media, algorithms, big data, robotics, and artificial intelligence (AI) – pose to themselves, to their society, and to democratic processes and institutions? Is the current wave of education reforms – labeled as "neoliberal" by some – that has spread across the world likely to prepare students for a difficult-to-predict world of new technologies? Given a rapidly changing commercial world, are we positioning students to learn-on-the-go as existing jobs are transformed or disappear and new jobs emerge? Are the widely touted "21st-century skills" sufficient preparation for this new world? What of other conceptualizations of the skills and dispositions believed needed for the future, ideas such as science, technology, engineering, and mathematics (STEM) (or science, technology, engineering, arts, and mathematics [STEAM]), "socio-emotional learning," "deep learning," and "soft skills"? How and where are the young to learn these? Do these capture the skills, knowledge, and dispositions that a highly uncertain future requires?

Further questions that interest us include: How are our students being introduced to the world in which they will need to make a living and to live, we hope, satisfying lives? How are they to engage with society? How do they protect and promote democratic institutions and values such as civil liberties, justice, respect for others, and inclusivity? How do they view others, particularly those who hold different values, beliefs, and customs? How do they work to reconfigure globalization for the good of all and not just the favored few? How will they reconcile resurgent nationalism with the imperative to collaborate globally to address existential threats such as climate change and debilitating economic and political inequities?

These are some of the questions we will attempt to address with a deep sense of humility engendered by uncertainty and recognition of the limits of our knowledge. We also recognize that there are many who have a greater understanding of the issues we attempt to address. Yet, our beliefs and commitments compel us to offer our assessments of the challenges the future will pose to current and future students. To wait until we felt we had the depth of knowledge and understanding required for more definitive conclusions and suggestions would mean this project would likely never be completed before we checked out of our mortal coils. And just as climate scientists describe the "inflection point" for climate change after which damage is irreversible, we feel that perhaps we are reaching an inflection point for education. We worry that current systems may not provide the experiences and learning opportunities necessary to cultivate on a large scale the innovative, iconoclastic, and generative thinkers and creators needed for a future that nourishes the minds, bodies, and spirits of everyone.

With trepidation, we offer some ideas about learning opportunities and educator roles that may have the potential to bring about the changes needed. Some of these involve "unschooling," long a marginalized and criticized vision of how to better support the development of skills, knowledge, and moral values in the young. We worry that the inherent "grammar" of schooling is difficult to change significantly and inhibits the larger project of developing people who are creative, caring, socially minded, skilled, inquisitive, intellectually flexible, and skeptical. At the same time, we have faith that there are many educators who, given the right resources, support, and opportunities, can create experiences that will engage, inspire, and embolden their students. This is what, ultimately, makes us hopeful about the uncertain future.

Our Intended Audience

Our hope is that students, parents, educators in both the P–12 and higher education worlds, and policymakers will read this book and discuss the questions and issues that we raise. We have attempted to write this book for a broad audience as we believe all of us need to be part of the conversation. We all play critical roles in providing our youth with the education they will need for an uncertain and rapidly evolving world.

Organization of the Book

In Chapter 1, we argue that the future is both increasingly difficult to predict and evolving at a pace never previously experienced. Jobs and whole industries are disappearing while new jobs and industries are born. In addition, social media, AI, big data, virtual reality (VR), and so on are changing faster than we can monitor and control. One result is that societies have become fractured. Aiding and abetting these fracrures are social media that benefit from misinformation and controversy even as they profit from selling our poersonal informantion.

Given the lack of agreement on how to control the depredations of social media, our only recourse is better educating our students about the manipulators behind the curtain.

In Chapters 2 and 3, we describe potential futures: one bright and one dark. In the bright future, technology makes our lives even more convenient and productive. Becoming less dependent on jobs for income could enable us to allocate more of our time to activities that feed our mind, body, and spirit. The dark future could evolve out of failures to address gross inequities in wealth and opportunity, climate chaos, and violent conflicts. This is a future in which the right to privacy has been completely eroded and unaccountable entities control access to information. This is a future in which we have failed to provide the support and opportunities students require to control their fate and that of their societies.

In Chapter 4, we look at the future of how work and workers will be organized. We look at various trends that are likely to be influenced by evolving technologies and social norms. As organizations become flatter, opportunities and expectations for workers change. Teams become the norm and capitalizing on the benefits of diversity is a necessity. Technology is also accelerating trends toward more remote work, entrepreneurship, freelancing, gig work, and side hustles. We also describe the qualities, dispositions, social behaviors, and skills that are likely to advantage students in the future.

We challenge the idea, in Chapter 5, that machines will replace virtually all humans in the future, given that we are uncertain about what new enterprises and activities as-yet-to-be-invented technology will spawn. We argue that it is a mistake to assume that the skills, knowledge, and dispositions that suited an industrial age are what is needed for the future. In Chapter 6, we focus on the potential of technology to revolutionize education in ways that will better position students for an uncertain future. We also explore how technology can free teachers from time and effort devoted to routine and curriculum coverage, to assume roles that are potentially more satisfying and supportive of their students' learning.

In Chapter 7, we describe the rethinking we believe is necessary for our students to be prepared to create a future that is more equitable, secure, productive, and satisfying for all, not just a privileged few. We close with an invitation to students, families, educators, and policy-makers to engage in a conversation about how best to prepare our youth for an uncertain future.

References

Anderson, M. & Jiang, J. (May 13, 2018). Teens, Social Media and Technology 2018. https://www.pewresearch.org/internet/2018/05/31/teens-social-media-technology-2018/

Lustgarter, A. (July 23, 2020). Where will everyone go? *ProPublica*. https://features.propublica.org/climate-migration/model-how-climate-refugees-move-across-continents/

McDonald, J. (2014). *American school reform*. Chicago, IL: University of Chicago Press.

McLaughlin, M. (2014). Storefront revolutionary: Martin Sostres Afro-Asian bookshop, black liberation culture, and the new left, 1964–75. *The Sixties*, 7(1), 1–27. doi: 10.1080/17541328.2014.930265

National Education Association of the United States (Committee on Secondary School Studies). (1894). *Report of the committee of ten on secondary school studies: With the reports of the conferences arranged by the committee*. New York: American Book Company.

1

Uncertainty

Why Is the Future So Hard to Predict?

Among the most popular Sunday comics from the last century was Dick Tracy. He was the lantern-jawed, trench-coated, fedora-wearing detective who always got his man. What was most fascinating was the communication device he wore on his wrist from the 1940s on. Not only could he talk to other cops but – at least after 1964 – he could also see them. No doubt, most readers at the time could not imagine a future in which Dick's technology would become a reality. Fast forward 50 years and, sure enough, if you've got the money, you can have a reasonable facsimile of Dick's device that does even more than communicate. You can use it to adjust the temperature in your home, spy on newly hatched chicks in your bird box, and take your blood pressure and send the results to your doctor.

That such a device is now on sale speaks to how the stuff of science fiction is becoming part of everyday life – at least for those with the wherewithal to afford such gadgets. Disruptive technologies have, of course, appeared periodically across history, but the rate of technological change has accelerated. Between the introduction of Watt's steam engine in 1763 and the electric motor in 1835, 72 years passed. Thirty-eight years elapsed between the advent of the telegraph and that of the telephone in 1876. Marconi patented the radio in 1895 but commercial radio did not take off until 1921, amplified in the mid-1920s by the advent of vacuum tubes that, in turn, spurred the development of television. The first commercial TV broadcast happened in 1939. In 1952, universal automatic computers (UNIVACs) went

DOI: 10.4324/9781315682884-2

on sale. Thirty years later, *Time* magazine's "Man of the Year" was the personal computer (PC). Fourteen years after that, the Blackberry arrived, the iPhone 11 years after that, and the Apple watch 7 years later.

Compared to earlier disruptive technologies, computers have evolved at a breathtaking rate. The 1960 census was analyzed on a UNIVAC 1105 computer that occupied the entire ground floor of Phillips Hall Annex at the University of North Carolina. The UNIVAC weighed in at a hefty 19 tons, sported dozens of vacuum tubes, diodes, and transistors, and required a 35-ton air-conditioning system to keep it from melting down. Today, of course, that UNIVAC is to the smartphone as an ox cart is to an F-16.

The magnitude of the impact these changes have had on our lives is matched only by the speed of the change. Extrapolating from the present even to the relatively near future is extraordinarily difficult. Some far-sighted prognosticators may have foreseen personal computers and handheld devices. But how many foresaw that within two decades after the arrival of PCs we would be carrying in our pockets devices with computing power as great as, if not greater than, many PCs (not to mention the 16-ton UNIVAC)? While technologies such as smartphones and smartwatches have evolved from earlier hardware, these are not simply extensions of previous technologies but reconceptualizations.

Innovation at Warp Speed

The speed of evolution and innovation is, it seems, outpacing our capacity to evaluate the impact on our social, psychological, and political lives. We didn't have the opportunity – or the needed information – to decide whether the benefits of platforms such as Facebook and Twitter outweigh the dangers. They appeared and, willy-nilly, unregulated, they grew like exponentially. The uses of the platform for not merely connecting but also, among other things, facilitating the creation of political "echo chambers" seem to have caught Facebook off guard. The filtering mechanisms for content proved ill-designed to weed out dangerous information. As its founders claim, it was not prepared to be an arbiter of free speech.

As a consequence, we as parents, citizens, and educators are left to react after the fact. At the risk of sounding like modern-day Cassandras, we think our education systems are lagging well behind the evolution not only of emerging technologies but also the social, economic, and political consequences of these technologies. More generally, government agencies appear ill-equipped or unwilling to regulate social media to protect children from bullying or prevent violence.

Information and communications technology (ICT) courses and units are becoming ubiquitous on school syllabi across the world as well as on pan-national curricula such as the International Baccalaureate. Policymakers around the globe rank the development of digital skills on a par with reading and math. Yet, we know little about how educators are engaging students in critically evaluating these technologies. How many educators challenge students to consider how social media, online retailers, and service providers, and news, information, and entertainment sites collect and use the data they unwittingly provide? We know little about how educators help students develop the capacity to evaluate the validity of news and information readily available online.

Lacking a fundamental understanding of the world of big data and algorithms, students are susceptible to manipulation as consumers of products, information, and ideas. The internet gives a whole new meaning to Twain's quip that "a lie can travel half-way around the world while the truth is putting on its shoes." Now, it can travel completely around the world in less time than it takes to find your shoes. Not only are our education institutions struggling to keep pace with the evolution of devices and the tidal wave of digital content, but they are also under pressure to prepare students for a world of work that is evolving in ways that are more unpredictable than ever before.

Future of Work

As a teenager, Pulitzer Prize–winning journalist Carl Bernstein, who would later help bring down a mendacious president (no, not the 45th – rather the 37th), spent more time in the local pool hall than in school. His exasperated father told him that if he wasn't going to school, he needed to get a job. Through a friend at the *Washington Sun* newspaper, the elder Bernstein helped his son land a job as a copy boy. What, you may be wondering, is a "copy boy"? Prior to the arrival of computers, journalists would compose their stories on typewriters. When ready, they would shout, "Copy!" and a fleet-footed youth would grab the copy and shuttle it to an editor who would polish it for publication. The young Bernstein instantly fell in love with the frantic energy of the newsroom (the *Sun*, in the 1950s, published *five* daily editions!), and the rest – as they say – is history.

Copy boys as well as typesetters and other newspaper workers have gone the way of saddle shoes and ducktail haircuts. Smoked-filled newsrooms humming with the sound of clacking typewriters, the chatter of reporters, and the ringing of phones have given way – as Bernstein noted – to carpeted offices indistinguishable from those of law firms.

The US Labor Department reports that, between 1990 and 2016, the newspaper business lost 60% of its jobs – from 458,000 to 183,000. In that same period, however, internet publishing and broadcasting rose from 28,800 to 197,800 – a 587% increase. Unfortunately for hard-copy newspapers, these trends continue. Between 2016 and 2020, internet publishing and web portal employment increased another 48% while newspaper publishing lost an additional 38% of the remaining jobs. Technologies giveth and technologies taketh away.

This is critical to think about the future of jobs. As industries such as print newspapers decline, new industries and jobs appear. Copy boys give way to coders as stories flow through digital editorial programs to arrive at news sites.

The issue is less whether or not jobs will be available for students of today as well as in the future and more whether we are preparing students for as-yet-created jobs and lifetimes in which they will change jobs frequently. The model of schooling and, to some degree, the curriculum we have are largely relics of the industrial age when jobs were stable and most workers worked in the same industry all their lives.

As we noted, the world of work is morphing more rapidly than ever before in history. What do the jobs on this list have in common?

- Social media manager
- Digital marketer

- Wind energy engineer
- Data miner/data scientist
- Search engine optimization expert
- Application developer
- Cloud specialist
- Digital course designer
- Massive open online course (MOOC) coordinator/instructor

If you guessed they are all newly created jobs, you would be right. These jobs didn't exist a couple of decades ago. Now, guess what these jobs have in common:

- Telecommunications line installers and repairers
- Installation, maintenance, and repair worker helpers
- Production worker helpers
- Chief executives
- Order clerks
- Data entry keyers
- Bill and account collectors
- Postal service mail sorters, processors, and machine operators
- File clerks
- Telemarketers

These are the most rapidly disappearing jobs in the United States, according to the Labor Department occupational employment statistics. That new technologies are predictably replacing manual and lower-skilled jobs such as repair worker helpers and file clerks is not a great surprise. To see chief executives on the list, however, is a puzzler. According to a *Governing* magazine article, there were 106,000 fewer chief executives in 2019 than a decade earlier.

A common assumption is that manual and low-skill jobs will be the first to disappear. The data suggest this may be true – but white-collar jobs are also disappearing at historic rates. If corner office jobs are disappearing, what other "highly skilled" jobs may be at risk? This suggests that technological innovations are likely to disrupt the world of work and organizations in ways that are not easily predicted.

Of course, business experts are busily reading all the tea leaves they can gather to foretell the future of work. For instance, McKinsey estimated, in 2017, that only about 5% of current jobs could be fully automated and, in 60% of occupations, about a third of the tasks could be automated. Looking into the future, McKinsey researchers estimated that by 2030, roughly 15% of current tasks could be fully automated although this estimate will vary by country as the costs of automation are significant. Not only is the initial cost of robotics considerable but ongoing maintenance also adds to the long-term cost. The upshot is that many jobs will not disappear but will be reshaped substantially by technology, requiring workers to master new skills and to possess a flexible mindset that regards relearning and retraining as normal and expected. The Columbia School of Journalism Review reports that although 25,000 print journalists lost their jobs between 2005 and 2015, the number of reporters at digital-only providers tripled.

Where will employment likely expand according to McKinsey?

- healthcare providers
- professionals such as engineers, scientists, accountants, and analysts
- IT professionals and other technology specialists
- managers and executives, whose work cannot easily be replaced by machines
- educators, especially in emerging economies with young populations
- "creatives," a small but growing category of artists, performers, and entertainers who will be in demand as rising incomes create more demand for leisure and recreation
- builders and related professions, particularly in the scenario that involves higher investments in infrastructure and buildings
- manual and service jobs in unpredictable environments, such as home-health aides and gardeners

(McKinsey, 2017)

Using US Labor Department data, McKinsey prognosticators estimate that, by 2030, automation will displace 400–800 million workers who will need to find new jobs. They compare the likely future workforce transformation to that caused by the shift from agricultural to industrial economies in the late 19th century in the West and in the 20th century in other countries (McKinsey, 2017).

The Organization for Economic Cooperation and Development (OECD) has looked at the likely future scenarios for European workers. The OECD estimates that, by 2030, 22% of current jobs will be automated and half the European workforce will have to transition to new or reconfigured jobs (OECD, 2017). OECD experts reiterate a point made by McKinsey: most jobs will require workers to collaborate with some form of advanced technology – robotics, artificial intelligence (AI), big data, and on. This underlines the importance of basic digital literacy for all students.

Pandemic Effects

Although it is too early to determine just how the dislocations caused by lockdowns will affect jobs in the long term, one thing is apparent: the effects of the pandemic will likely accelerate current trends. McKinsey's survey of 800 business executives revealed that the adoption of robotics, driverless vehicles, digitization and the use of AI have grown significantly during the pandemic and they expect this to continue post-pandemic (McKinsey, 2021). The OECD reports similar findings, noting that 25% of the labor market will need "reskilling" by 2025, changes that the pandemic accelerated (OECD, 2021). According to the OECD, acceleration has occurred in three major areas: remote work, digitization, and automation. Jobs that were gradually morphing as organizations and individuals capitalized on emerging technologies have transformed almost overnight and most are unlikely to return to the status quo ante.

Although susceptible to their own species of viruses, robots, unlike many humans, are immune to Covid-19. Compounding existing inequities, the jobs hurt most by Covid-19 are usually filled by workers with the lowest educational levels. This hampers their ability to shift to new jobs that require higher-level skills and knowledge. McKinsey estimates that workers with no higher education tend to occupy jobs that are twice as likely to be at risk due to the virus as those filled by university graduates (McKinsey, 2021; Smit et al., 2020). This hastens the trend for jobs already most at risk for automation: 24 million

European jobs are estimated to be at risk from both automation and Covid-19. Yet, fewer jobs in Europe are as vulnerable to Covid-19-related decline as are at risk in the United States – 26–35% of the total labor force (Smit et al., 2020). In short, the pandemic has highlighted the need to rethink the knowledge, skills, and mindsets that today's students will need as they enter the job market. Moreover, the pandemic has acted as an accelerant for transformations in the job world. To catch up, schools and classrooms need to change more quickly than ever before imagined. Sadly, rapid change and adaptation have not been defining characteristics of education in the United States and elsewhere.

Organizations and Work

Adobe Analytics reported that pajama sales between November 2019 and November 2020 jumped 200%. Hilarious – as well as just plain embarrassing – stories of Zoom *faux pas* pop up online every minute or so. Did you hear the one about the woman whose boyfriend let rip a bong hit in the background while she was on a video call with her boss and co-workers (she claimed it was the dishwasher – which is even funnier)? Or the guy who relieved himself in the adjoining bathroom without muting himself? Or the elementary teacher who inadvertently farted during her Zoom class? Needless to say, hilarity ensued among her third graders.

Many people around the world are having to learn new ways of working and collaborating from home. What had been a gradual trend for some has become a necessity for many. Data from the Federal Statistical Office show that workers, even before the pandemic, working from home for at least half a day per week increased from 18% to 24% between 2013 and 2018. During the current crisis, at least half of all employees and the self-employed are working from home. Many of these – perhaps more than a third – do not envision returning to their workplaces when the pandemic is over.

The downsides of the trends for future jobs are many. Bernstein's newsroom was not merely a workplace. It was a hive of interactions. In addition to the conflicts that arise in virtually all social settings, the folks in the room experienced connectedness and interdependence.

They communicated not just verbally but also through body language and facial expressions. Sitting alone in your room, looking at the faces of your students, family members, friends, classmates, or co-workers on a screen will never be the same. For too many, the pandemic has exacerbated feelings of loneliness and isolation. Unknown is whether the growth in online communities during the pandemic will translate into similar in-person communities once gatherings are safe. If the present is a prelude to the future, inventing new ways for humans to socialize may be critical. This trend toward isolation predates the substitution of digital for in-person interactions, as Robert Putnam argued in *Bowling Alone* and may have contributed to the increasing tribalism we see in the United States (Putnam, 2001).

Educating for Uncertainty

This leads us to the central questions of this book: How do we educate students for a future fraught with uncertainty? How do we equip them to deal with new technologies that impact their social, work, and political lives? How do we prepare them for jobs and organizations that have yet to be created? How do we prepare them to transition as smoothly as possible from one job to the next, from one industry to the next? How do we help them become the independent learners they will need to be? How do we help them learn to engage and collaborate with others in healthy, sustaining, and productive ways, inside and outside the digital world? How do we support them as they craft their identities and look for meaning in their lives?

In later chapters, we revisit some of the list of skills and knowledge some organizations have proposed that the future requires. Here, we wish to engage readers in imagining a future whose outlines are fuzzy, at best, and in reimagining education for such a future. Few times, if any, in the past have we been less sure about what the future holds. The sheer speed and variety of technological evolution require us to step back from our current mode of thinking about learning, knowledge, and teaching. The uncertainty and unpredictability of the future have deepened during the pandemic.

Driving the educational policies in many countries is the belief that to compete, students must be prepared for the "knowledge economy"

(Roberts, 2009). From this perspective, the primary purpose of education is to develop a country's human capital, in particular, the cognitive capabilities of its workers. These cognitive capabilities are believed to be the key to the innovations that countries believe will spur economic growth and gain them a competitive edge in the world economy. Increasingly, countries prize the creation of intellectual property that underlies technological innovations.

The question is: How ready are schools, as presently configured, to develop students' capacities for a rapidly evolving world of work and participate in the knowledge economy? Are they capable of helping students learn what may be of greatest value to them in this new world of the future? Are schools capable of providing opportunities for students to become the innovative thinkers necessary to thrive in an economy that differs significantly from the past? Some teachers are already looking beyond the requirements of the conventional school curriculum. They understand that preparation for the future requires engaging students in ways that differ from the past. Yet, despite decades of research on learning and teacher training courses devoted to the learning sciences, many classrooms look much as they did in decades past. We know that many students do not learn well from this type of conventional pedagogy. Yet, this illustrates the staying power of what has been termed the "grammar of schooling" that plays out in classrooms around the world: a teacher stands at the front of the room holding a textbook with students sitting in orderly rows, heads bent over their own textbooks (or, in some cases, digital device), many of them wishing they were anywhere but where they are required to be (Tyack & Tobin, 1994). Despite attention given to the "knowledge economy" and its reliance on innovation, most students continue to be subject to a steady barrage of information in the hopes that somehow this will help them develop their cognitive capabilities. Why is that the case?

The answer is, in part, captured by the words of a teacher of English we interviewed at an elementary school in Nantong, China. Nantong is a medium-sized city of 7.2 million just north of Shanghai with a prosperous harbor and a fast-growing population. After the teacher described a typical teaching day that includes five one-hour classes with 40–50 students in each, she expressed her frustrations. "We do know what good practice in language teaching is. But our performance is judged by how our students do on the standardized test." She produced a test booklet on which was printed such questions as: "Insert the correct adverb in the following sentences..."; "Which of the following punctuation marks are misplaced...?"; "Rearrange the following words to make a complete sentence." She went on to explain that if students don't perform well on the tests, parents as well as administrators blame – and sometimes shame – the teachers.

Like many teachers, this teacher knows better ways of helping her students master useful knowledge and skills, and understands research on second language learning. However, she feels hemmed in by a system that, above all else, values performance on exams that require memorization. "Critical thinking," the ability to apply knowledge and innovate, though watchwords for educational reforms and leaders, is not tested. Not tested translates to "not valued" in current education systems. That such systems will cultivate in diverse students the intellectual capabilities that are widely believed critical to the future seems highly unlikely.

Proponents of the need to prepare students for the knowledge economy – including the World Bank, the OECD, International Monetary Fund (IMF), and so on – also emphasize the need for schools and educators to be held accountable for student performance. This translates into a greater reliance than ever before on external measures of student performance such as the Programme for International Student Assessment (PISA) and Trends in International Mathematics and Science Study (TIMSS). A shared belief among policymakers worldwide is that success on these measures is a prerequisite for economic success, although no evidence for such a causal relationship exists. Rather than acknowledging that future uncertainties require a rethinking of education systems, policymakers have, in a sense, doubled-down on an old formula: require students to demonstrate their ability to reproduce existing bodies of knowledge and blame the schools for poor results.

We are arguing that the rapid evolution of technology and the uncertainties of the future place a premium on ways of thinking, habits of mind, self-monitoring, and collaboration that schools as currently conceived are ill-equipped to develop. Calls for 21st-century skills that emphasize broader skills and capabilities abound, yet how schooling must be reconfigured and policies changed to cultivate both cognitive and non-cognitive skills have been largely unheeded. When confronted with the need to address new areas of knowledge and skills, education yet institutions – higher education as well as schools – typically respond by adding to the existing curriculum, contributing to cognitive overload for students.

As teacher education programs came under pressure because the mostly White teaching force proved largely unprepared to work successfully with non-White students, they responded by adding multicultural courses to the curriculum. Similarly, some schools responded to the call for teaching "critical thinking" by adding classes or units on the topic. Such responses give the appearance of addressing these issues without having to fundamentally rethink the educational enterprise. Both of these issues speak to what some would argue is the heart of education: ensure that all students succeed in an increasingly globalized future.

Students' Critical Capacities

Perhaps even less well foreseen than our new devices is the use to which they are being put. Who foresaw the explosion of social media and the effects it would have on our personal, professional, social, and political lives? Friends and family stay in touch, share moments of joy, humor, and grief. Organizations such as non-profits and churches share information and recruit donors and members. Businesses, large and small, advertise and tout their products. Artists display their creations. Singers sing and dancers dance. We find others who share our interests, beliefs, values, concerns, fears, and hopes. We find old friends, colleagues, and long-lost relatives. We find confirmation and validation.

That is not all, of course. Someone throws out into the ether a seemingly far-fetched fever dream: Hillary Clinton is running a pedophile ring out of a DC pizza restaurant. Shortly afterward, a guy shows up and begins shooting up the place. A group of hackers congregate in a warehouse in St Petersburg and generate thousands of fake accounts to influence the outcome of the 2016 election. A 13-year-old commits suicide because of online bullying. Again, who foresaw such happenings?

These consequences of the internet and the proliferation of social media were unforeseen by, at most, a handful of technological oracles. Social media illustrates both the benefits and dangers of technologies that continue to evolve. TikTok, Twitter, and Instagram challenge YouTube and Facebook for "eyeballs." WhatsApp, WeChat, and Messenger connect us and provide additional channels for sharing information, opinions, and ideas as well as misinformation and outrage as do online forums such as Reddit and Quora. What new platforms will emerge offering what affordances is, again, difficult to foresee.

As we are witnessing, the ends to which rapidly evolving technological tools are put are beyond control once the tech-genie has escaped the app-store lamp. Some of these are more obvious than others. Some appear benign to youthful users but are, in fact, dangerous. Many users are unaware of the extent to which they are being influenced, often subtly, through their use of these media. Every keystroke represents a data point. Every "like" is registered, sorted, and available for analysis and exploitation (Goodman, 2016). As we are, say, checking out new cookware online, an ad pops up for Game of Thrones paper dolls. We think to ourselves, "Now, how did they know I have a thing for Sandor Glegan?" And, of course, the algorithms used to analyze our data are tuned to ensure we return again and again to our favorite sites. The more often we return, the more data we provide, the more data we provide, the better algorithms can identify our tastes and needs, the better algorithms can offer things to meet our tastes and needs, the more often we return, and on it goes. Somewhere, B. F. Skinner is smiling.

Understanding the digital underbelly of social media and other platforms is not enough, however. Perhaps more important is students' capacity to evaluate what they see, and hear, and to find. And evaluate the evidence behind claims and assertions they encounter online. Never has this been more essential. Recently, Facebook removed 1,700 pages, 5,600 groups, and 18,700 Instagram accounts identified as part of the QAnon conspiracy network. Among other bonkers accusations, QAnon followers claim that the Democratic

Party and the "deep state" are actually at the core of a pedophile and sex-trafficking ring that kidnaps children to harvest their adrenaline to create andrenochrome that Hollywood elites then use to rejuvenate. Yeah.

Most disturbingly for us as educators, all of these QAnon followers presumably went to school and most, at least, graduated from high school. How did we, as educators, fail them? From the Founders to the early public school advocates to Dewey and down to the present, the critical link between education and democracy has been an underlying rationale for the existence of public schools. Dewey argued that democracy requires an informed and knowledgeable citizenry equipped to critically evaluate choices and make decisions for the good of the whole. In other words, citizens need the capacity for both logical and moral reasoning.

Although some people will, for various reasons, always be more susceptible than others to conspiracies, lies, distortions, and so on, helping students develop their capacities to reason logically and morally is vital to their present and future. While the capacity for logical and moral reasoning is inherent, those in our environment – family, peers, religious leaders, teachers, media, and so on – are also shaping these capacities. Expecting these influencers of youth's reasoning capacity to begin using verified evidence and moral precepts such as compassion for one's enemies (a precept embraced by all major religions) as bases for decisions is a pipe dream. Consequently, we need to revisit the role of educators in helping students develop their reasoning capacities – both logical and moral.

Although this has long been a goal of many educators, the uncertainty presented by the future supports the contention that these should be the primary foci of education. As new technologies appear at an ever-increasing rate, people will need to be able to weigh the potential costs and benefits, foresee unintended consequences, and assess the impact on the common good. How should we think about prenatal gene therapy? Clearly, addressing genetic disorders has the potential to benefit families and society as a whole. However, what about genetic enhancements? This illustrates the types of issues that are likely to confront people increasingly as new technologies – in medical as well as other fields – emerge.

Summary

We began this chapter arguing that much of our current technology was unforeseen. New technologies that are likely to emerge over the next few decades are also likely to be unimagined. This uncertainty about the future has profound implications for how we are preparing our youth not only as future workers but also as productive members of society who live fulfilling and contributive lives.

Because of the speed of technological developments, some current jobs will disappear but new jobs will emerge. Today's students can expect to experience four or five different careers – not just different jobs within the same industry but new jobs in new fields. This raises critical questions about how we are equipping students with not just the cognitive but also the non-cognitive capabilities and skills required.

In addition, digital technology has become the primary vehicle for disseminating news and information (and misinformation) with, in some cases, potentially dangerous consequences. Through digital platforms, we provide data about ourselves that large companies monetize as we lose control over our privacy. The question is: Does the increasing emphasis on ICT in schools worldwide include addressing the threats that digital platforms and sellers pose? This is related to the larger question of whether schools are currently suited to helping students become the critical lifelong learners that reform advocates promote. And, ultimately, the question we all must face is: Who's in charge – technology or us?

In the chapters that follow, we look more closely at the rapid evolution of jobs and workplaces, accelerated by the pandemic, and the implications for what students need to be learning now. We offer contrasting pictures of the future – one in which conveniences enable us to enjoy life more fully and one in which most people will struggle to survive and find meaning in their lives. We then look at how work is likely to be organized in the future as the economy changes. We also return to the issue of why schools and education are so darn hard to change – a question scholars and educators have pondered for decades. We then revisit the skills, knowledge, and dispositions that the future is likely to require. We end with thoughts on how teaching, learning opportunities, assessments, and schools may need to change if we are to prepare our students for an uncertain and unpredictable future.

To reiterate: our purpose is not to prescribe as much as to provoke and engage others in the questions and possibilities we raise. As economist and philosopher Frederick Hayek (1960) observed:

> It is because every individual knows so little and, in particular, because we rarely know which of us knows best that we trust the independent and competitive efforts of many to induce the emergence of what we shall want when we see it.

As Hayek notes, we do not know who knows best. Hence, the need for a conversation to induce "what we shall want when we see it."

References

Goodman, M. (2016). *Future crimes: Inside the digital underground and the battle for our connected world*. New York: Anchor Books.

Hayek, F. (1960, October). *The case for freedom*. Foundation for Economic Freedom. Retrieved 03/05/2021 from: https://fee.org/articles/the-case-for-freedom/.

McKinsey (2017). *Jobs lost, jobs gained: What the future of work will mean for jobs, skills, and wages*. Retrieved from www.mckinsey.com/featured-insights/future-of-work/jobs-lost-jobs-gained-what-the-future-of-work-will-mean-for-jobs-skills-and-wages.

McKinsey (2021). *What 800 executives envision for the postpandemic workforce*. Retrieved from: www.mckinsey.com/featured-insights/future-of-work/what-800-executives-envision-for-the-postpandemic-workforce.

OECD (2017). How technology and globalisation are transforming the labour market, in *OECD employment outlook 2017*. Paris: OECD Publishing. Retrieved from: https://doi.org/10.1787/empl_outlook-2017-7-en.

OECD (2021). 5 things to know about the future of jobs. Retrieved from: www.weforum.org/agenda/2020/10/5-thing-to-know-about-the-future-of-jobs.

Putnam, R. (2001). *Bowling alone: The collapse and revival of American community*. New York: Touchstone Books.

Roberts, J. (2009). The global knowledge economy in question. *Critical Perspectives on International Business*, *5*(4), 285–303. Retrieved 03/05/2021 from: www.academia.edu/359426/The_global_knowledge_economy_in_question.

Smit, S., Tacke, T., Lund, S. Manyika, J., & Thiel, L. (2020, June). *The future of work in Europe*. McKinsey Global Institute. Retrieved from: www.mckinsey.com/featured-insights/future-of-work/the-future-of-work-in-europe#:~:text=A%20discussion%20paper%20by%20the%20McKinsey%20Global%20Institute%2C,will%20continue%20to%20do%20so%20in%20the%20future.

Tyack, D. & Tobin, W. (1994, fall). The "grammar" of schooling: Why has it been so hard to change? *American Educational Research Journal*, *31*(3): 453–479.

2

The Bright Side of the Future World

"Andrew would implement the Freedom Dividend, a universal basic income of $1,000/month, $12,000 a year, for every American adult over the age of 18" (Yang, 2020). Andrew is the former Democratic presidential and New York mayoral candidate Andrew Yang. During the US 2020 presidential election, Yang proposed the idea of the Freedom Dividend, a form of universal basic income (UBI) for all Americans. The idea is simple: the government would send a check for a certain amount of money to its citizens every month or every year.

Various forms of UBI have been proposed and tested in history and around the world. Sir Thomas More's *Utopia* describes a state-run basic income system in the 16th century. Subsequently, many politicians, economists, and philosophers proposed different forms of UBI. Dr Martin Luther King argued that the guaranteed income should be implemented to abolish poverty in the 1960s. As unlikely as it seems, Richard Nixon proposed instituting a guaranteed basic annual income of $1,600 (about $10,000 in today's dollars) in 1969, an idea his advisers convinced him to scrap. The idea has also been piloted for short periods of time and/or in reduced forms in different places around the world. While arguments and debates remain, the idea has certainly become increasingly popular in recent years. In the United States, over 30 cities have been pushing for universal income in 2020 (Hess, 2020). In April, 2021, Congress approved direct payments to families with children of $300 for each child under six years old and $250 for each child six to seventeen years old. These benefits

DOI: 10.4324/9781315682884-3

are phased out for married couples or widows/widowers earning more than $150,000, heads of households earning more than $112,500, and $75,00 for others. Some view this as a significant step toward UBI, especially given that conservative Senator Mitt Romney had earlier proposed just such child benefits.

Technological changes have spurred an increased interest in the idea that is also seen as a way to address the widening wealth gap. Over the past few decades, technology has advanced enough to displace millions of people from their jobs. It has rendered obsolete some industries and created new possibilities. With further development in the near future of artificial intelligence (AI), robotics, and associated technologies, many more jobs will be automated. The Fourth Industrial Revolution (Schwab, 2015) is likely to leave an increasing number of people jobless. Although future technologies will generate new jobs, whether these will be sufficient to offset the jobs that will disappear remains to be seen.

Another possibility is that human beings may not need to work as much. If UBI were to become a reality, human beings could receive a livable income without having a job. If you think making a living without having to work is a wonderful thing, more wonderful things could further brighten the future. Without having to work, you would have the time to do more or less whatever you wish. Although we cannot predict with any certainty how this might unfold, we can sketch a possible future scenario.

Living in a globally connected network, you can potentially communicate with anyone anywhere in the world via video, audio, or text or a combination of all three. You can start the day enjoying a conversation with a friend or a group of friends from different parts of the world. You may, in fact, invite friends to a virtual conversation and project their holograms into your living room. After the conversation, you might invite your virtual friends to watch videos with you on YouTube or some other yet-to-be-created platform. Videos you might choose could simply be entertainment: funny, mesmerizing, inspiring, sobering, or sad. Or they could be educational or instructional. After watching some videos, you may text invite another friend to meet you, face to face, for coffee at a nearby cafe.

You text a car service and, shortly, a driverless car arrives to take you to the cafe. On the 20-minute ride, you can choose music or video, enjoy a back massage from the automated seat, or video chat with friends. A robot wearing a green apron greets you as you enter the cafe, another prepares the drink you have ordered from the car, and a third delivers it to your table along with a pastry and a jaunty, "Enjoy!"

After coffee, you and your friend decide you will shop in-person for a bit rather than order online and wait at home for the delivery drone. At a nearby clothing store, a smartly dressed robot greets you and your friend, asks how you are, and, in a melodious voice, suggests you look at a new shipment of hats that are on sale. You notice a human, clearly the manager, interacting with the sales clerk robot. The manager approaches and offers her assistance. You decline politely and peruse the hats, occasionally using your phone to scan possible purchases to discover and compare the price with other vendors. Having made your choice, you scan the tag and pay with the app on your phone. As you leave, the sales clerk robot hands you a bag for the hat. You bid your friend goodbye, contact a driverless car via a phone app, and return home, your new hat perched on your head.

This story could continue, sketching life as it might be in the not-so-distant future. The story could have multiple versions, depending on the person in the story, but the underlying theme is a future in which working for a living is largely a relic of the past. In this future, technology will have replaced many more humans and will provide more services and conveniences to humans. What's happening in the story is actually not that far from reality. Much of the technology in the story has been realized or tested in lab situations.

The future can be bright. The brightness of the future comes from a series of potential technological advances that include ethical or green creativity and technological development, just socioeconomic policies, peaceful power balances in geopolitics, and thoughtful environmental and public health actions. If the right decisions are made, human beings could enjoy a prosperous, peaceful, and healthy future. (This is, of course, a major "if.") The bright future is characterized by increased convenience, choices, human connections, and health.

Increased Convenience

Technological changes have made human life much more convenient than ever before. Already we can travel just about anywhere by automobiles, planes, trains, and so forth. We can shop online and have goods delivered to our home. We can take courses online and learn anything we like. We can turn on our phones and choose from millions of songs to listen to, watch any one of millions of videos online, or catch up on news from around the world. We can chat or video chat with friends who live on the other side of the globe. We have washing machines, dishwashers, air-conditioners, microwaves, and refrigerators. We needn't wait for newspapers to be delivered as Google delivers the news to our screens or, if we prefer, we can watch or listen on our devices. We needn't visit a bookstore to buy the latest bestseller. We can download it or listen to the audio version. Most of us have more than we need for a convenient life.

And more is coming. Technological changes continue at a dizzying pace, bringing even greater convenience. In 2019, *Time* published a story about a robot, Stevie, in a senior community in Washington, DC (Purtill, 2019). The robot was made by the Robotics and Innovation Lab at Trinity College, Dublin. The lab was interested in understanding how robots can assist with the work of caring for elderly people. Taking care of the elderly has become a big issue for many countries, including the United States, where people over 65 are the fastest-growing age demographic. But the eldercare workforce is not growing to keep pace with demand. The *Time* article estimated a shortfall of 151,000 paid workers by 2030, a gap that is expected to increase to 355,000 by 2040. The absence of qualified professional caregivers means that family members and friends have to step in at great cost to their own financial and physical health. The Trinity College lab developers reasoned that perhaps AI-based robots can play a role in filling the gap in needed carers for the elderly.

Stevie is an example. Robots can do many things in senior communities. Robotic exoskeletons can help staff lift patients safely. Delivery robots can zip around hospital hallways like motorized service carts. Therapy robots can comfort and calm patients who have dementia. Robotic dispensing systems can also work with pharmacists to fill prescriptions – and reduce the incidences of inadvertent medication mistakes. They can monitor elders and alert staff when a patient needs help and can also provide entertainment, singing, dancing, reading, and storytelling for patients. Robots like Stevie, which was designed as a socially assistive robot, can play games with patients and provide companionship. They can also remotely engage isolated elders in conversations.

Stevie is not unique. A group of researchers at Stanford University studied robot use in nursing homes in Japan and found that over 60% of nursing facilities employed robots in 2020 (Oliver Wyman Forum, 2020). These robots have become a necessity in performing all sorts of jobs, especially during the Covid-19 pandemic.

Stevie is just another example of how technology provides more convenience and services. The convenience and service that robots have brought to elders and the disabled can also happen in other places where such services are needed. Robots can work in homes, restaurants, bookstores, shops, and hospitals. They can do a lot of things that make living more convenient and comfortable and alleviate the suffering of vulnerable groups. Examples of technology providing convenience and support will doubtlessly emerge in the next few years and decades.

Increased Choices

Technology has greatly increased our choices that could make the future brighter. Human beings prefer to have choices. Most of us commonly owned only one television set. Now, many of us have multiple video screens that allow us to watch TV channels, stream movies and videos, play games, and follow the news. Not that long ago, we were limited to just a handful of TV channels. Now, hundreds are available (including a Norwegian channel devoted to logs burning in a fireplace). Watching TV is no longer confined to TV sets. We can now watch on phones, tablets, and computers. Not only can we watch TV on our phones, tablets, and computers, but we can also choose from hundreds of thousands of videos. On YouTube, 300 hours of video are uploaded every minute and nearly five billion videos are watched each day.

Videos are just one example of the hugely increased choices we now enjoy. The same has happened with books, songs, music, podcasts, and video games. Self-publishing is a major force enabled by today's technology. Any individual can create and share content globally. Anyone in the world can, given the resources, have a website, blog, YouTube channel, Facebook page, or podcast to disseminate whatever they choose. These sites are globally available to virtually everyone, although some countries do restrict access to content that their government deems dangerous, immoral, or provocative. Anyone can create videos of their music performances, dance, opinions, kids, police actions, cats, and so on (the possibilities are almost endless) on their phone, tablet, or computer and upload them to globally accessible platforms. This capacity has greatly expanded the choices both as creators and consumers that we enjoy today.

Other choices have also increased dramatically. Physical goods such as clothing, electronics, furniture, tools, even coffins can be bought online, making it possible for any designer, creator, or manufacturer to market their products to customers globally. Likewise, choices in food have increased. We can purchase food and ingredients online from anywhere in the world. Not only can we choose from multiple makes and models of automobiles but we can also customize our choices (heated seats? surround sound? rear-view camera? touchscreen? parking assistance? Wi-Fi? sunroof? blind-spot video?).

Increased choices make it possible to cater to individual preferences and to allow individuals to personalize their life experiences. Many have taken advantage of the advanced technology to personalize their access to news, stories, music, and entertainment on news portals, video platforms, and music sites. But more exciting and life-saving things are happening. Personalized medicine (PM) is one such field (Vogenberg et al., 2010).

For those who can access it, PM is a way to deal with the problems created by a one-size-fits-all approach to diagnostics, drug therapy, and prevention. Despite our biological similarities, humans differ in critical ways. Pharmaceuticals and treatments interact differently depending on an individual's physiology, genetics, history, race, and so on. The same medicine may be very effective for some patients but can trigger serious side effects in others. Finding the right medicine for the right condition for the right person is critical.

In PM, physicians use a profile of a patient's gene variations to guide treatments that ensure more successful outcomes and minimize harmful side effects for the patient. PM can also help with prevention by indicating a person's susceptibility to certain diseases before they become manifest. This enables physicians and their patients to design a plan for monitoring and prevention. Essentially, PM allows physicians to go beyond the one-size-fits-all model of medical treatment or diagnosis to make more effective decisions for each individual patient (Vogenberg et al., 2010).

PM has not reached everyone yet, but the revolution has begun. Real-world examples have shown that PM is shifting the emphasis in medicine from reaction to prevention, enabling the selection of optimal treatment, and reducing trial-and-error treatments, making drug use safer by avoiding side effects, reducing the time and cost of clinical trials, and lowering the overall cost of health care. PM relies on both scientific and technological advances. New tools are available to decode the human genome faster, more cheaply, and more accurately. Large-scale research studies link genetic variations to diseases and conditions across many countries. Aggressive new investments are fostering technological developments that spur the integration of research and clinical data.

Increased Connections

Another indicator of a bright future is increased connections. Human beings are social animals. We are driven to connect. For thousands of years, geography restricted human connections. For much of human history, we made friends – and enemies – and maintained relationships within a limited area. We have been working on solving the distance problem since the beginning of humanity. Animals such as horses, donkeys, camels, and dogs helped travel on land. Sea vessels shrank distances by water. Steam and, later, electric and combustion engines dramatically changed the situation enabling travel by air and rail, shortening distances between humans. Communication technologies such as the telegram, telephone, radio, television, and the internet turned the world into a global village, no longer bound by the limitations of physical travel.

Today, physical distance is not the barrier to human connection it was for most of our history. Before the Covid-19 pandemic, human movement across geographical borders was prodigious. Internationally, airports logged nearly 1.5 billion arrivals in 2019.[1] The pandemic has slowed human movement but with vaccines and more control of the virus, human beings will eventually resume their travels and movement. Even the pandemic did not completely shut down human interactions. On the contrary, interactions among humans have increased.

The increase has been very largely online. Predictably, humans took advantage of online communication affordances to interact. These interactions span the gamut of our activities. We used online tools to maintain friendships and family bonds, teach classes, conduct meetings, and attend conferences and concerts online. We managed our work teams, businesses, and organizations online. A dean at a major US university told us she had been in 8 hours of Zoom meetings by 14:00. Webinars on a range of topics are now commonplace.

Where possible, numerous companies, large and small, moved their work online. An acquaintance told us his team logged onto Discord (a platform originally for gamers but repurposed during the pandemic) at 09:00 and remained online across the day. He occasionally spoke with the whole group and met with individuals separately in chat rooms as needed. Nearly 50% of white-collar work has reportedly moved online and may stay there after the pandemic (World Economic Forum, 2020). As a result, the number of Zoom users and users of other online synchronous meeting platforms grew from 10 million in December 2019 to over 300 million in April 2020.

The increased interactions among people, enabled by technology, afford us multiple opportunities. First, any of us can interact with anyone with access to communication technology anywhere on the globe or even in outer space. Astronauts on the international space station routinely communicate with people on earth. Second, we can interact with others through a variety of media – video, audio, graphics, text, or a combination of all. Third, we can interact synchronously and asynchronously. Finally, our interactions can include even very large groups of people.

The increased interactions have had a tremendous impact on all aspects of human life. In politics, social media has played an increasingly important role. Groups of people who share political opinions form their own communities and develop their own strategies to influence elections and public opinions. In the United States, social media may have a greater impact, rightly or wrongly, than traditional media. In economics, people have created and participated in economic activities online through connections with investors, customers, designers, developers, and manufacturers. Social media has also become one of the largest employers in the world. Facebook and Twitter, for example, employed nearly 50,000 workers in 2019. This does not include the individuals who advertise their products and services via social media and other platforms such as Amazon, eBay, Reddit, Etsy, and app stores.

The increased connections also make it possible for people to make friends with people from distant places, expanding their circle of acquaintances. This creates opportunities for people to learn the perspectives and ideas of folks different from themselves. Through online multiplayer video games, gamers connect and interact with people they may never have met nor will ever meet and may live halfway across the globe. They may end up collaborating with gamers with whom they share little beyond their passion for the game.

Connections enable opportunities for learning that never before existed. Massive open online courses (MOOCs) have been around for more than a decade but enrollment in online courses exploded during the pandemic. A major provider of online courses, Coursera reported that enrollment grew 640% from spring 2019 to spring 2020.[2] With Covid-19-related school closures, some parents have created social media–supported learning pods – parents working together to hire mentors for their children. The number of online book clubs, large and small, has skyrocketed as have cooking and crafting online groups.

The Big Picture

These trends suggest the positive roles that technology can play in shaping the future. Overall, the threat of dying from starvation, exposure, war, or disease is less than ever for the majority of people on the planet. In fact, most of us are likely to live longer than past generations because of advances in medicine and diminished war casualties. Most of us have more and more human connections. This bright future, however, offers even more.

The hope is that collective international actions can at least slow, if not stop, the deterioration of the climate. The Paris Agreement set a promising example of global cooperation. Participating parties (countries, territories, and independent political entities) number 188, representing more than 90% of the world's countries. The goal is to keep the global temperature rise well below 2°C above pre-industrial levels. It is also to limit the temperature increase to 1.5°C. If this were achieved, our climate would not be a threat to humanity; it could become otherwise.

Other environmental threats could also be controlled. Sea-level rise could be controlled to reduce the threat to coastal cities and low-lying regions. Erosion of ecological diversities could be stopped or at least slowed. Natural disasters such as earthquakes, hurricanes, and tsunamis would be less devastating, saving lives and limiting destruction. Diseases would be easier to control and future viruses would be better contained than was the case with Covid-19 in 2020.

The bright future includes the possibility that increased international cooperation would forestall violent conflicts. Nations will certainly continue to compete, but they would abandon armed conflict as the way to resolve disputes and achieve their goals. Major powers will avoid not only nuclear war but also war itself. The disputes and disagreements that seem inevitable among countries as well as the actions of non-state terrorist groups will continue to cause death and destruction but on a relatively small scale by historical standards. By and large, however, nations will focus on economic productivity, the well-being of their people, and productive competition rather than on military aggression.

Making the Future Brighter

This bright future, of course, is yet to be realized. It is not waiting just over the horizon for our children. Instead, this is a future, if it is to be realized, that our children must create with our help, guidance, and support.

As we noted at the start of this projection of the "best of all possible worlds," concepts such as UBI have the potential to reshape the future. For it to become a reality requires diligence across multiple domains including politics, economics, and sociocultural values. Politicians, especially in the United States, cannot simply decide to give unattached money to every citizen (although the state of Alaska does exactly that, annually providing each residence with a permanent fund dividend check – most recently for $992). They must carefully consider the consequences, intended and unintended, of such a policy. They must also determine where the money will come from and if the economy can support it. Among the considerations is the extent to which automation and robots will replace human beings, necessitating some form of public assistance for displaced workers. They also need to determine if guaranteed incomes will sap recipients' incentive to find work, as some critics claim. Critics also warn that safeguards may be needed so payments are not used for illegal activities or contraband such as illicit drugs.

To make UBI viable, we also need an economy that evolves in a direction that supports such a policy. An economy that continues to rely heavily on human labor undercuts arguments for UBI. As the prevalence and sophistication of machines progressively transform the job sector of the economy, the need for UBI will become increasingly urgent. More and more people will be unable to find even subsistence-level work, thereby requiring subsidies just to survive.

The prospect of UBI also raises social and cultural questions. For example, if everyone is eligible to receive a basic income, does it mean nobody will want to work? No matter how technology evolves, societies will still need some people to work. For those who are not working, the question is: How will they spend their lives? How will those who work regard those who don't? Currently, in countries with robust social welfare systems, workers often resent beneficiaries of the dole whom they regard as slackers despite evidence that most welfare recipients face multiple obstacles to getting full-time jobs.

These are a few of the many questions that proposals for a UBI raise. To address these and other issues will require a collective effort involving not just experts – economists, psychologists, sociologists, philosophers – but all citizens to participate and voice their views. In societies such as the United States, leaders will have to address concerns arising from deeply held beliefs about the role and importance of work and the responsibilities of the government. UBI is just one example of the possibilities likely to arise if we are all engaged in crafting a more inclusive, equitable, and democratic society for the future.

The other dimensions of the bright future – increased convenience, choice, connection, and harmony – are in many ways already a reality for the majority of people living in developed countries and a small group living in less-developed countries. Today's students will need to have the knowledge, skills, and dispositions to manage dimensions of the future. Perhaps most importantly, we need to figure out how to spread this bright future to people across the globe as well as within national boundaries. To leave some people behind is fundamentally unethical. As Dr Martin Luther King wrote in his *Letter from Birmingham Jail*, "Injustice anywhere is a threat to justice everywhere. We are caught in an inescapable network of mutuality, tied in a single garment of destiny. Whatever affects one directly, affects all indirectly." Recently, the spread of Black Lives Matter protests around the world is an encouraging expression of the mutuality about which Dr King wrote. As the only privileged person on an impoverished block, you cannot count on your wealth to guarantee safety and happiness for yourself much less for the neighborhood. An imperative for the future is to ensure that prosperity, justice, and peace are shared by all.

Secondly, the technology that brings us convenience, choice, connection, and harmony can also bring us inconvenience, limited choices, constrained connections, and disharmony in tandem. In other words, we could also be facing a dark future, a future in which human beings suffer from isolation, conflict, and violence, widening inequities and poverty, and horrible environmental consequences. Like an evil twin of the bright future, this dark future is also in the making at the moment, perhaps even smirking at the optimism of this chapter. In the next chapter, we describe the dark sides of the future.

Summary

The future world can be very bright, with a universal basic income for everyone, with global connections with friends and families, with easy and wonderful technology assistance for shopping and living, and with personalized medicine and robotic assistance in life. This future can happen with technological development and sound, supportive policies. Whether technology evolves in a beneficial direction and policies focus on the well-being of all rather than a privileged few depend on the people we educate who will be the creators of the future. They will direct the development and use of technology and decide how future technology will affect the lives of people and the planet. The question for educators is how best to prepare students to manage evolving technologies in ways that contribute to a bright future for everyone.

Notes

1 www.statista.com/topics/962/global-tourism/.
2 https://theconversation.com/massive-online-open-courses-see-exponential-growth-during-covid-19-pandemic-141859.

References

Hess, A. J. (2020, Jan 19). Meet the mayors pushing for guaranteed income in 30 cities across the country. *CNBC*. Retrieved from: www.cnbc.com/2021/01/19/the-mayors-piloting-guaranteed-income-programs-across-the-us.html.

Oliver Wyman Forum (2020). Robots may be the right prescription for struggling nursing homes. *Oliver Wyman Forum*. Retrieved from: https://www.oliverwymanforum.com/city-readiness/2020/jun/robots-may-be-the-right-prescription-for-struggling-nursing-homes.html.

Purtill, C. (2019, October 4). Stop me if you've heard this one: A robot and a team of Irish scientists walk into a senior living home. *Time*. Retrieved from: https://time.com/longform/senior-care-robot/.

Schwab, K. (2015). The fourth industrial revolution: What it means and how to respond. *Foreign Affairs* (December 12). Retrieved from: www.foreignaffairs.com/articles/2015-12-12/fourth-industrial-revolution.

Vogenberg, F. R., Isaacson Barash, C., & Pursel, M. (2010). Personalized medicine: part 1: Evolution and development into theranostics. *Pharmacy and Therapeutics (P&T)*, *35*(10), 560–576. Retrieved from: https://pubmed.ncbi.nlm.nih.gov/21037908; www.ncbi.nlm.nih.gov/pmc/articles/PMC2957753/.

World Economic Forum (2020). *The future of jobs report 2020*. Retrieved from: www3.weforum.org/docs/WEF_Future_of_Jobs_2020.pdf.

Yang, A. (2020). *The freedom dividend*. Retrieved from: www.yang2020.com/policies/the-freedom-dividend/.

3

The Dark Side of the Future World

The Covid-19 pandemic has been a global catastrophe. Over 44 million people lost their jobs in the United States, driving the country's unemployment rate to about 15% in April and June 2020. But some people, the ultra-rich ones, enjoyed tremendous growth in their wealth. The combined wealth of billionaires in the United States increased by more than $637 billion to a total of $3.6 trillion, more than the entire wealth of 54 countries in Africa. The fortunes of the top five billionaires increased by 26%, which was a whopping $102 billion (Goldin & Muggah, 2020).

Since the 1970s, the income gap has been widening in the United States. The top 1% of Americans has nearly doubled their share of the national income over the past five decades, while the official poverty rate for all American families has barely moved. From 1993 to 2018, the top 1% earners' income growth was 100.5% but only 18.3% for the bottom 99% (Saez, 2020). As a result, about 40% of the total US population either is poor or has low income.

Growth in the income gap is not only in the United States but also global. There is a growing disparity between developed and developing countries. The world's richest 1% own 44% of the world's wealth, while more than 56% of the world's population own less than 2% of the global wealth, surviving on less than $10,000 a year. Those who own $100,000 and over make up less than 11% of the global population but own more than 80% of the world's wealth. The share of the national income going to the top 1% has increased rapidly since 1980 in North America, China, India, Russia, and Europe, although more

DOI: 10.4324/9781315682884-4

moderately. Covid-19 has made the situation worse. According to a survey of 37 countries, more than three in four households reported an income loss during Covid-19. Worse, the impact is more significant on the poor. More poorer families reported income losses than those not classified as poor (82% vs. 70%) (Edwards, 2020). The Covid-19 pandemic may have pushed at least an additional 100 million people into extreme poverty and acute hunger doubled to 260 million people in 2020 (Goldin & Muggah, 2020).

The growing income and wealth gap between the wealthy and the poor creates extreme tension for human society. It has created a divided world and our future is likely to be a divided one, with social unrest and extreme tensions between the rich and the poor. Unless changes are made to ensure that prosperity is shared by all people, it is possible that the division will continue to make the human world a miserable place.

An Unequal Future

Today's world has enough inequalities. These inequalities are likely to grow in the future. In 2011, the Stanford Center on Poverty and Inequality published *20 Facts about U.S. Inequality that Everyone Should Know* (Stanford Center on Poverty and Inequality, 2011). Using a variety of data, the center highlights some of the biggest problems in equity in the United States. For example, since the 1980s, wage inequality has grown significantly with upper-tail inequality increasing steadily. Chief executive officer (CEO) pay increased from 24 times the average production worker in 1965 to 185 times in 2009. In 2019, the average top CEO compensation was $14.5 million, which is 320 times the typical worker (Mishel & Kandra, 2020).

The income gap between male and female workers is another fact noted by the Stanford Center. Women made about 60% of the income of men throughout most of the 20th century. In the late 1970s, women saw a substantial increase in their income, bringing it up to 80% of men's income. But since 2005, the income gap has remained unchanged (Stanford Center on Poverty and Inequality, 2011). In 2020, the gap remains about the same, with women making about 82 cents for every $1 earned by men (Bleiweis, 2020).

The wealth and income gaps among different racial groups in the United States are huge. According to the Inequality.org website, the median African-American family, with about $3,500, owns just 2% of the wealth of the nearly $147,000 the median White family has, while the median Latino family, with about $6,500, owns just 4% of the wealth of the White family. In other words, the median White family owns 41 times more wealth than the median Black family and 22 times more wealth than the median Latino family. Black and Latino families are also much more likely than Whites to have zero or negative wealth. From 1983 to 2016, the percentage of Black families with zero or negative wealth rose from 8.5 to 37 and the percentage of Latino families with zero or negative income is more than twice that of Whites. In terms of income, the median White worker made 28% more than the median Black worker and 35% more than the Latino worker (Inequality.org, 2020).

Inequality goes way beyond income and wealth. It also happens in areas such as job opportunities. For example, the unemployment rate for Black jobseekers is nearly twice as high as for Whites (Inequality .org, 2020). A study carried out in Chicago and Boston in 2001 and 2002 found that resumes with "white-sounding" names, whether male or female, were much more likely to have callbacks for interviews than were those with "black-sounding" names (even though the resumes were otherwise identical) (Stanford Center on Poverty and Inequality, 2011).

Globally speaking, inequalities are large as well. There are large gaps not only within nations but also among nations. A number of very obvious inequalities among nations are listed on *Our World in Data*: the average income in the richest country Qatar is 177 times more than the poorest country the Central African Republic ($117,000 vs. $661). The United States has a gross domestic product (GDP) per capita of $54,000, which means more than 6 years of spending in the Central African Republic; a child born in the worst health countries is 60 times more likely to die than a counterpart born in the best health countries; children in poor countries can have up to 5 years of education while those in rich countries about 20 years of education (Roser, 2020).

There are many different indicators of inequality and there is a substantial amount of different evidence to support the existence and increasing inequality among different groups of people in different countries. Covid-19 has exacerbated the situation. Poor workers may suffer more in the pandemic and women also have lost more job opportunities during the pandemic. The basic story is that we are very likely to live in a world of inequalities, which affects how we live and educate.

A Monitored/Naked Future (No Privacy)

In May 2019, San Francisco became the first city in the United States to ban the use of facial recognition technology by local agencies such as law enforcement and the city's transport authority (Lee, 2019). In September, 2020, the city of Portland, Oregon, banned the use of facial recognition technology by city departments and public facing businesses, representing the broadest ban in the country (Metz, 2020). Many US cities such as Oakland and Boston have issued such bans since Portland and it is expected that more cities will follow suit.

This ban is surely the right thing for governments to do, but individuals in modern society should not expect that the banning of facial recognition in cities will solve the problem of being naked in the world. We are all essentially under the watch of modern technologies.

Facial recognition is one of the most obvious monitoring technologies. China has perhaps the most advanced facial recognition technology in the world and has been using it without much concern. China has had 350 million cameras installed, which means one camera for every 4.1 persons, and this number is expected to reach over 560 million by 2021, which will be the largest share of surveillance cameras installed globally (Ricker, 2019). These cameras have been used generously by the police and other government authorities in addressing public security and political issues.

Despite the various city bans, the United States actually has about the same ratio of camera to person as China. With over 70 million cameras installed in 2018, the ratio was about one camera for every 4.6 persons in the United States. Other top camera jurisdictions include Taiwan (1:5.5), the UK and Ireland (1:6.5), and Singapore (1:7.1).

Besides cameras that watch the movement and recognize the faces of individuals on the streets, other data about an individual make him or her visible globally. One's personal data – date of birth, place of birth, social security numbers or other identifying numbers, bank accounts, home addresses – have been collected in many forms by different agencies. They are stored on various computers and can be easily misused for identity theft and marketing purposes. Numerous cases of data theft have happened to millions of people. During the Covid-19 pandemic, cyberattacks have been on the rise, and health systems have seen increasing threats to their patients' data (Ford, 2020). There has also been an increase in personal data being stolen from government and business systems.

Moreover, recent years have seen the growth of DNA testing. Companies such as 23andMe have started marketing DNA testing kits directly to customers, enabling the user to see how they may be genetically related to different ancestry groups. These companies collect the data of millions and then sell them to different health and medical systems and companies, which can use the DNA to develop new medicine. Of course, police and other organizations can use the DNA to track potential criminals. The capture of the infamous Golden Gate killer Joseph James DeAngelo was largely due to a public genealogy website that provided DNA data. In the future, companies can use DNA data for various other possibilities such as tracking terrorists, providing insurance company data about potential customers, and possibly for employers to use the data to decide whom to hire. There can be more disastrous and beneficial uses. However, imagine what a global company that has the DNA data of all humans can do to human beings?

A Divided Future

One of the largest problems we will face in the future is the continuation or worsening of the income and wealth gap. This gap will not only leave too many people in poverty and misery but also increase the existing divisions among people in a country and among countries of people who have been at odds with each other. The division of people has come to exhibit its ugly side in recent years.

Take the United States as an example. There is no question that the country is divided. Former President Donald Trump, for example, never accepted President Joe Biden's victory in the 2020 presidential election. He even incited an insurrection on the US Capitol while his own Vice President Mike Pence was counting votes in Congress. Moreover, about 88% of Trump voters believe Biden did not win the election legitimately, without evidence (Walsh, 2020). Biden's win was not a landslide, with 306 electoral votes, but it was a legitimate win. The number of Biden voters is about six million more than Trump voters, out of a total of about 150 million voters.

The division in political views in the United States is expressed in many different ways. There were widespread protests in 2020 following the killing of George Floyd in Minneapolis. These protests called for the acknowledgement of and action to end historical and systemic racism. At the same time, plenty of counterprotests were organized and held by those who did not believe that the American system is racist. White supremacists were rampant and held strong.

Technology has played a significant role in dividing the nation. Brookings Institution visiting fellow Tom Wheeler writes that "digital technology is gnawing at the core of democracy by dividing us into tribes and devaluing truth" (Wheeler, 2020). He points out that "[s]ocial media undermines what the Founding Fathers were focusing on when they wrote 'We the People' and established the motto 'E Pluribus Unum' (out of many, one)" (Wheeler, 2020). While democracy requires human beings to overcome inherent and innate tribalism, "the business plans of the dominant digital companies are built on dividing us into tribes in order to sell targeted access to each tribe" (Wheeler, 2020).

Social media was supposed to connect people but it has left people isolated and tribal. Facebook was supposed to be a digital platform that connects old friends and family members, but it has become numerous tribes of different opinions and interests. Twitter, Instagram, and Pinterest have done the same. Social media, broadly speaking, uses algorithms to send advertisements, information, news, and the names of users to interested people. Thus, the more one person is interested in one category of things or one set of ideas, the more likely that he or she will receive information concerning that category or set of ideas. Recommendations of other users who have similar interests will also be made to him or her. In the end, after numerous iterations, the person will have a circle of "friends" who agree with him or her and receive mostly information that he or she likes. As psychiatrist Arash Javanbakht and digital marketing expert Maryna Arakcheieva write in *Psychology Today*:

> This is how one's Matrix can become the extremes of conservatism, liberalism, different religions, climate change worriers or deniers, or other ideologies. Members of each tribe keep consuming and feeding one another the same ideology while policing one another against opening up to "the others."
>
> (Javanbakht & Arakcheieva, 2020)

Tribalism is commonplace today. In the United States, people with a different political or ideological interest receive their news from different sources. News sources have become very diverse and extreme, especially with self-media. There are also "fake news" sources that simply spread rumors and false information. Nonetheless, they can all be treated as news sources online. Additionally, many people no longer trust traditional media. They only believe in their friends or what passes through the internet.

This division has significant implications for real life. For example, a study by the Pew Research Center found drastic differences between Republicans and Democrats in their views on the coronavirus. The study found that about two-thirds of Republicans believed that the virus was controlled as much as it could be, but 88% of Democrats disagreed. Furthermore, Republicans were much more likely than Democrats (68% vs. 15%) to say that the outbreak has been overblown. In contrast, 43% of Democrats say the pandemic has been made into a smaller deal than it really is, compared with only 9% of Republicans. More interestingly, the study tracked news sources and found that where one receives one's news matters a great deal. The study found that 90% of Republicans who only indicated Fox News and/or talk radio as their major sources of news believed the country has controlled the outbreak as much as possible. But only 46% of Republicans who rely on neither Fox News nor talk radio but rely on at least one of the other major news providers shared the same opinion (Jurkowitz et al., 2020).

The division in the United States is also seen elsewhere in the world. In Europe, conflicts among racial and religious groups have been on the rise. Protests on the streets and terrorists activities have increased. The UK has been in the fight over Brexit for the past 4 years. France has been dealing with protests and terrorist attacks. Germany has also been in the midst of polarization between the Far Right and the Far Left (Volk, 2020). Other European countries have been divided by different opinions about immigration, Muslims, and other social issues.

Not only are nations divided, but so too is the world. The United States and China, two of the world's most powerful economies, have been in a trade war. They are also in conflict in many other areas such as diplomacy, science and technology, and even education. Two consulates, one for each, have been closed. The US–China conflicts have also involved other countries such as Australia, the UK, and the European Union. In addition, China has been struggling with India over its borders and other countries in the South China Sea. If no military action is taken against each other, this battle may be called another Cold War.

The divided world makes it very difficult to conduct civic duties. It has made civil debates and discussions almost impossible. Societies have become groups of isolated tribes who endorse one another but exercise extreme hostility toward others. But democracies require conversations and debates to function. Sound policies cannot come from polarized parties or divided people. It is thus necessary for the divided people to come together, to be unified, and to have civil debates and discussions. Division is dangerous for everyone involved.

The division in the world is also unproductive. Trade wars, military conflicts, and sanctions ultimately don't make the world a better place. Human beings need to move goods, information, money, and people across national borders. Such movement, when appropriate and following the laws, is essential for a more peaceful and prosperous world.

A Jobless Future

Three years before the Covid-19 pandemic hit, McKinsey published a report in 2017. The report suggests that one-third of the activities in 60% of occupations could be automated. It concludes that by the year 2030, about 10 years hence, between almost 0% and 30% of the hours worked globally could be automated (Manyika et al., 2017). In 2019, a World Economic Forum article suggested that the McKinsey prediction of a total loss of 800 million jobs or one-third of the world's jobs might be too high. The author, Jayant Menon, a lead economist at the Asian Development Bank, and adjunct fellow of the Crawford School of Public Policy, the Australian National University, argued that previous revolutions had similar predictions about job losses, but in the end there was an increase (Menon, 2019). The point is perhaps not necessarily about job losses or gains because that happens when technology is introduced. The point is about retraining and reskilling existing workers for new tasks.

Predictions about job losses or gains are interesting but they are rarely accurate for a number of reasons. First, automation is here and certainly displaces human workers. That is, existing tasks can be and have been replaced. However, a person's job can have multiple tasks. When one task is replaced, the job may still exist but acquires new tasks. Human beings invent technology to do their tedious, heavy, and unpleasant work. This is true, for example, for nursing home workers who work with robots. Robots can help lift patients but they do not replace workers.

Second, machines can replace human workers in some occupations but they also create new jobs. For example, automated teller machines (ATMs) and phone banking technology have replaced many bank tellers but they have also created jobs for people to design, develop, and manage the ATMs and new banking technologies. Driverless cars will make millions of truck drivers and taxi drivers unnecessary, but they will also create jobs for computer programmers and new car designers.

Third, technology can destroy existing professions but can also create new ones. Online shopping has made small, local stores disappear but at the same time has created a huge workforce of deliverers. This is why companies such as UPS, FedEx, and Amazon and many logistics companies have created millions of part-time and full-time jobs around the world. This is also why Airbnb, which has caused a decline in hotel workers, has created many jobs for people to manage and take care of rentals.

Fourth, technological advances can lead to the creation of new industries and new jobs. Technological revolutions are supposed to be disruptive. They are supposed to bring new possibilities and potentials. In terms of jobs, they may make traditional industries completely irrelevant. But at the same time, they create completely new jobs. These jobs may not be known or predictable but they do emerge. Previous revolutions have completely transformed agriculture, for example, but created massive factories.

While it may not mean much to predict job losses or gains as technology moves forward, it is meaningful to emphasize that technological advances do place human beings in awkward positions, especially when technology changes are rapid, like today. When technology moves forward rapidly, jobs change fast. A person's work life may span 40 years, and if technology does not change fast and jobs only change every 50 years, the person will not need much change in his or her expertise or knowledge. However, if technology leads to job changes every 5 years, the person will have to be trained or reskilled every 5 years just to keep his or her job.

Today, technology changes rapidly, making it impossible for a person to hold on to the same job without being retrained every few years. Thus, the future may be jobless for those who are unwilling or unable to be retrained. The future could be jobless for our children who do not have the skills and knowledge required to enter the new world.

Our scenarios suggest that by 2030, 75–375 million workers (3–14% of the global workforce) will need to switch occupational categories. Moreover, all workers will need to adapt as their occupations evolve alongside increasingly capable machines. Some of that adaptation will require higher educational attainment, or spending more time on activities that require social and emotional skills, creativity, high-level cognitive capabilities, and other skills relatively hard to automate.

A Fragile Future

The future may be very fragile. Given the increasingly digital connections we rely on, everything could disappear in a matter of seconds or minutes. Water, electricity, and sewage systems are all connected and managed by digital networks. If a group of individuals with bad intentions gained access to these systems, they could turn them off or introduce bad codes remotely, causing massive damage to our daily lives. Likewise, with automatic cars, manufacturing devices, and robotics, the wrong person could stop them or move them as he or she wishes. Airports, airplanes, train systems, subway systems, and other transportation systems could also be hijacked and controlled by criminals or terrorists, who could turn all functioning systems into horrific human disasters. These may not happen, but they could happen. If technology is used to support these systems, they can be infiltrated and controlled by people other than those who are in charge of them.

The fragility of the future applies to other aspects of human life. Banking systems, for example, are targets of many cyberattacks. Today, online banking is not an exception but the norm. In some countries, cashless currency is becoming the norm. If and when all societies' money is stored in online banking systems, the danger will greatly increase. Not only could all the money be stolen, but also a dictatorial government could seize the funds of individuals online. Despite the claims of their proponents, cryptocurrencies, like all things digital, are also vulnerable.

There are, of course, other opportunities for the world to collapse or, at least, face very challenging times. Many technological advances will present ethical and moral challenges to humanity. For example, genome or gene editing are technologies that provide the ability to alter an organism's DNA. These technologies enable genetic material to be removed, added, or altered in a genome. While it looks like these technologies have great potential to cure disease, they could also cause tremendous damage. Moreover, could they be used to manufacture new organisms or alter human beings to the extent that new species emerge? A doctor in China recently altered the genetic codes of infants so that they would be born with immunity against HIV. However, his method was banned and he was punished. Should genome editing be allowed to do more?

The same can be said about cloning, a technique to make exact genetic copies of an organism. Since the first cloning of Dolly the sheep in 1996, scientists have cloned many other animals such as cows, cats, deer, horses, and rabbits. It will not be long before scientists develop a procedure to clone human beings (they may already be able to do so). Should that happen? What if a non-state individual decides to clone a human army? Will countries have the ability to stop such actions?

These ethical issues are widespread and touch upon a lot of technological development in the future. They are emotional and quickly ignite furor across different groups. They are potentially lucrative because they can mean huge profits for companies, individuals, and nations. They are also political because they can drive different agendas in societies. They can, of course, be military with the power to wipe out enemies. All these issues make the future extremely fragile as well as unpredictable.

Summary

The future could be very dark. It could be a world with vast inequalities, resulting in disastrous social unrest and conflict among different groups of people. The recent conflicts in the streets of Paris and in many cities across the United States are just small examples of what could happen. A divided future could make it very difficult to govern, to fulfill civic duties, and to maintain a democracy. The possibility of an increasingly fragile world is a constant threat hanging over us. And living in the naked world, with all our information known to others, can be more than challenging. To live in this world requires us to rethink what we are, what we do, and how we live.

References

Bleiweis, R. (2020, March 24). Quick facts about the gender wage gap. *Center for American Progress*. Retrieved from: www.americanprogress.org/issues/women/reports/2020/03/24/482141/quick-facts-gender-wage-gap/.

Edwards, J. (2020). *Protect a generation: The impact of COVID-19 on children's lives*. Retrieved from: https://resourcecentre.savethechildren.net/node/18218/pdf/vr59-01_protect_a_generation_report_en_0.pdf.

Ford, P. (2020, August). Why a data security sting lurks in COVID-19's long tail. *Health Care News*. Retrieved from: www.healthcareitnews.com/news/emea/why-data-security-sting-lurks-covid-19-s-long-tail.

Goldin, I., & Muggah, R. (2020, October 9). COVID-19 is increasing multiple kinds of inequality. Here's what we can do about it. *World Economic Forum*. Retrieved from: www.weforum.org/agenda/2020/10/

covid-19-is-increasing-multiple-kinds-of-inequality-here-s-what-we-can-do-about-it/.

Inequality.org. (2020). *Facts: Racial economic inequality.* Inequality.org. Retrieved from: https://inequality.org/facts/racial-inequality/.

Javanbakht, A., & Arakcheieva, M. (2020, November 14). Social media, the matrix, and digital tribalism. *Psychology Today*. Retrieved from: www.psychologytoday.com/us/blog/the-many-faces-anxiety-and-trauma/202011/social-media-the-matrix-and-digital-tribalism.

Jurkowitz, M., Mitchell, A., Shearer, E., & Oliphant, J. B. (2020, October 7). Before Trump tested positive for coronavirus, Republicans' attention to pandemic had sharply declined. *Pew Research Center*. Retrieved from: www.journalism.org/2020/10/07/before-trump-tested-positive-for-coronavirus-republicans-attention-to-pandemic-had-sharply-declined/.

Lee, D. (2019, May 14). San Francisco is first US city to ban facial recognition. *BBC*. Retrieved from: www.bbc.com/news/technology-48276660.

Manyika, J., Lund, S., Chui, M., Bughin, J., Woetzel, J., Batra, P., Ko, R., & Sanghvi, S. (2017, November 28). Jobs lost, jobs gained: What the future of work will mean for jobs, skills, and wages. *McKinsey Global Institute*. Retrieved from: www.mckinsey.com/featured-insights/future-of-work/jobs-lost-jobs-gained-what-the-future-of-work-will-mean-for-jobs-skills-and-wages.

Menon, J. (2019, September 17). Why the fourth industrial revolution could spell more jobs – not fewer. *World Economic Forum*. Retrieved from: www.weforum.org/agenda/2019/09/fourth-industrial-revolution-jobs/

Metz, R. (2020, September 9). Portland passes broadest facial recognition ban in the US. *CNN*. Retrieved from: www.cnn.com/2020/09/09/tech/portland-facial-recognition-ban/index.html.

Mishel, L., & Kandra, J. (2020). CEO compensation surged 14% in 2019 to $21.3 million: CEOs now earn 320 times as much as a typical worker. *Economic Policy Institute*. Retrieved from: www.epi.org/publication/ceo-compensation-surged-14-in-2019-to-21-3-million-ceos-now-earn-320-times-as-much-as-a-typical-worker/.

Ricker, T. (2019, December 9). The US, like China, has about one surveillance camera for every four people, says report: One billion cameras will be installed globally by 2021, says IHS Markit. *The Verge*. Retrieved from: www.theverge.com/2019/12/9/21002515/surveillance-cameras-globally-us-china-amount-citizens.

Roser, M. (2020). Global economic inequality. *Our World in Data*. Retrieved from: https://ourworldindata.org/global-economic-inequality.

Saez, E. (2020, February). Striking it richer: The evolution of top incomes in the United States (updated with 2018 estimates). *UC Berkeley*. Retrieved from: https://eml.berkeley.edu/~saez/saez-UStopincomes-2018.pdf.

Stanford Center on Poverty and Inequality (2011). 20 facts about U.S. inequality that everyone should know. *Stanford Center on Poverty and*

Inequality. Retrieved from: https://inequality.stanford.edu/publications/20-facts-about-us-inequality-everyone-should-know.

Volk, S. (2020, November 16). What the Pegida movement tells us about divisions within German society. *European Politics and Policy*. Retrieved from: https://blogs.lse.ac.uk/europpblog/2020/11/16/what-the-pegida-movement-tells-us-about-divisions-within-german-society/.

Walsh, J. (2020, November 19). Poll: 88% of Trump supporters appear to falsely believe Biden didn't legitimately win. *Forbes*. Retrieved from: www.forbes.com/sites/joewalsh/2020/11/19/poll-88-of-trump-supporters-appear-to-falsely-believe-biden-didnt-legitimately-win/?sh=443fae037221.

Wheeler, T. (2020, February 7). Technology, tribalism, and truth. *Brookings Institutions*. Retrieved from: www.brookings.edu/blog/techtank/2020/02/07/technology-tribalism-and-truth/.

4

Organizations, Freelancing, Knowledge Creation, and Changing Norms

Recently, three millennial siblings discussed their work and workplaces. Brendan works at a very successful start-up, managing the coding team that is the backbone of the web-based business. Claire uses her design, cartooning, and illustration skills to land jobs in the gig economy as well as working as a nanny for three boys. Jamie works in a large-scale bakery, heading to work when many of us are just entering REM sleep, along with a work crew of mostly millennials such as himself.

Their work lives and workplaces differ significantly from those of previous generations. Brendan's team is part of a larger "scrum" that constitutes the way the business is organized. One scrum handles marketing, another production, another design, and another technology. Leaders of the scrums constitute the management team, each member of which is required to learn to code. This increases their understanding of the technological core of their web-based business. Every weekday morning, Brendan gathers his team of millennial programmers on Discord, originally a gamers' platform that has been co-opted to host meetings and other virtual gatherings during the pandemic. The team includes women, Asian Americans, and a gay male. He briefly reviews where the team is in completing its latest project and addressing any urgent tickets from other teams in the organization. The team members then move on to work on their tasks, remaining connected via Discord and, when needed, meeting in a virtual side room to discuss issues as they arise. Occasionally, Brendan or a team member may ask everyone to unmute themselves and turn on their video to discuss

DOI: 10.4324/9781315682884-5

a problem. Having the Discord platform open across the day allows for ad hoc conversations that research has found reassures workers of their importance to organizations.

As a team leader, Brendan is task focused, unconcerned if a colleague leaves to deal with a personal issue, eat, or even (gasp!) nap. If a problem arises with a team member's performance, Brendan's approach is to coach rather than reprimand. He knows that employees typically respond more positively to this approach (Robison, 2020). Over time, he has learned each member's strengths and weaknesses and assigns tasks accordingly. When appropriate, he tries to increase the capacity of team members by assigning tasks that require learning new skills. This helps keep them fully engaged and builds their resumes to improve their chances of moving up in the organization.

His team is well compensated and, Brendan believes, the members feel that the organization values them. If an emergency arises, the team works until the matter is resolved, regardless of the time involved. The company emphasizes agility, adapting to both internal changes and an evolving environment that the leadership monitors closely. Brendan works to keep his team similarly agile, prepared to respond quickly to changes within and outside the organization.

Brendan's team is like many others during the pandemic: nearly 57% of all teams are meeting remotely at least some of the time and 40% of these are, like Brendan's, exclusively remote (Ozimek, 2020).

Claire, on the other hand, is much like others among the more than 40 million gig workers. Her gig as a nanny assures her of a steady income (until her charges age-out of the need for a nanny) and frees her to pick and choose among design and illustration jobs that come her way, either from repeat or new clients. Although she must leave her home for her nanny job, she can pursue her design gigs from her little study with her cat on her lap.

In contrast, Jamie's workplace is more conventional: a large wholesale bakery. As he described his workplace to his siblings, the commonality that emerged related to workplace culture and norms. For Jamie, the appeal of his job, in addition to his interest in baking and food, is his co-workers who are mostly millennials. For him, comfort exists in being able to assume they share certain behavioral norms and cultural interests. Workplace issues common in prior generations simply do not exist for his work team, whether race, class, religion, or gender identification. If, for instance, someone asks their co-workers to use particular pronouns to represent their identity, that's their business. Everyone takes it in their stride. No need to get your MeUndies in a knot. Talk in the bakery revolves around the latest online games, music, podcasts, and Netflix as well as favorite hiking trails and outdoor bars. Self-deprecating humor is the currency of conversations. What some in older generations deprecate as "political correctness" is, for these workers, expressions of their beliefs and values. After work, a few may meet up online to play Rocket League or another multiplayer game. Through these contacts, he has also joined a Dungeon and Dragons group that gathers occasionally. Jamie says he feels no urgency at the moment to look for another job where he might use his BS degree in international studies. Although his wages are modest, so too are his needs. In addition, he would miss his co-workers and the comfort of his workplace were he to move on.

These three examples illustrate some of the important differences in work organizations as we look to the future: how organizations are being structured, how gig work is changing the job landscape, and how organizational behavioral norms and expectations are changing.

Organizational Structures and Remote Working

Many start-ups that flatten organizational hierarchies to facilitate the flow of information and ideas continued to thrive despite the Covid-19 pandemic. Evidence suggests that start-ups respond to changes in their environment more quickly than do traditional organizations. In fact, a recent study found that amid the pandemic the number of new start-ups increased 24% from 2019 to 2020 (Djankov & Zhang, 2021). The pandemic has also led to many more organizations encouraging or mandating working remotely although some jobs, especially those that are lower paying, still require workers to be physically present. This is especially true for healthcare workers.

As a result, many employees and employers have become more comfortable with remote working. Expectations are that when the pandemic has passed, some jobs will continue to be remote while others will become hybrid – some days in person, some days remote. As more organizations shift toward remote working, the possibility of extending their reach increases. Opportunities for new markets, hires, collaborations and joint enterprises, and information sharing expand globally.

Remote working also offers the potential for employees to experience a greater sense of agency. Brendan's team members have greater control over their lives and how and when they work than they did before the pandemic. As long as their tasks are done competently and on schedule and they are mindful that their colleagues' work may require them to meet certain deadlines, their work hours are flexible. The informality and equalitarian ethos of the organization encourages them to take the initiative and suggest creative solutions.

Of course, as the pandemic has taught us, remote work has significant downsides. It can lead to a sense of isolation and loneliness, a pre-existing problem that has been amplified by the pandemic (Sweet, 2021). Remote working doesn't afford the same opportunities for "accidental encounters" that employees experience in the office break room, experiences that offer vital human contact, contribute to a sense of connectedness, and can lead to sharing information and ideas. Remote work may also intrude into family life or the lives of others who share a living space. Finally, working remotely erodes the demarcation between work and leisure.

Despite these drawbacks, remote or hybrid work, made possible by digital technologies such as Slack, Zoom, Google Meet, GoToMeeting, Discord, and Skype, seems almost certain to continue to be part of our work experience in the future. Businesses and other organizations are finding they can save money on office rent and can tap a previously untapped global talent pool.

Contrary to the worries of some, evidence suggests that employees working remotely are more productive. An Airtasker survey showed that, while remote workers take more frequent breaks, they, in fact, spend more time on tasks than when warrened in their cubicles (Airtasker, 2020). Even before the pandemic, many workers said they would take a pay cut to be allowed to work from home. Finally, remote working may be good not only for businesses and workers but also for the planet: greenhouse gases dropped by about 10% in 2020 as travel in general fell dramatically.

The Gig Economy and Side Hustles Are Thriving

Those of us who grew up believing that a "steady job" working for the same organization was the key to prosperity and peace of mind are unlikely to be comfortable with Claire's reliance on gig work. As a freelancer, with a mortgage and car payments, she has a comfort level with uncertainty that many earlier generations would envy. For her, freelancing is not the last resort or a temporary solution to job loss. As with over 60% of her fellow freelancers, she prefers the flexibility and independence that gig work offers over the stability of a regular job. She knows that she can find work when she needs it. In fact, apparently 25% of freelancers are able to find a new gig within a day. How? Like many freelancers, sitting at her computer, a teacup steaming on her desk, she scrolls through the design and illustration jobs advertised on Upwork.com. If nothing there grabs her fancy, she might also check out the offerings on FlexJobs, SolidGigs, or the SubReddit community forum where freelancers and potential clients share possible gigs. Multiple sites exist to connect gig workers and side hustlers with, well, gigs. If Claire finds a gig that requires skills she may lack, she can use sites like InDeed to find other freelancers who have the needed skills she lacks and are interested in collaborating on a project. The downside of this is that she would have to share her earnings.

Of course, the gig workforce offers many other skills and services in addition to graphic design and illustration, including some that may be surprising and that are in greater demand than ever before. During the pandemic, the need for mental health therapy has skyrocketed. BetterHelp, TalkSpace, Regain, and several others offer online therapy with qualified therapists who are, in essence, gig workers. BetterHelp claims they add 10,000 new clients per day and some research has shown that online therapy may be just as effective as face to face – and a lot more cost-effective as well as safer during the pandemic. Online counseling affords greater privacy as well as convenience for both therapists and patients. A wholesale return to face-to-face counseling post-pandemic seems unlikely.

Tutoring, normally a face-to-face activity reaching back at least to Aristotle struggling to tame and teach the boy who became Alexander the Great, has gone online in a big way, a trend that pandemic-driven school closures escalated. Khan Academy, perhaps the best known of the online tutoring organizations, has been around since 2008. A non-profit like Khan Academy and established for-profit tutoring companies such as SmartThinking (Pearson) and Princeton.com have been joined by individuals and small groups that offer their tutoring services via the internet. Sign up with Wyzant and, if your qualifications check out, you could be tutoring tomorrow. The adult versions of tutoring – executive coaching and mentoring – have similarly grown online. Guru.com can match you in moments with a freelance executive coach or mentor. With the appropriate background and credentials, you can now coach or mentor from the comfort of your living room.

Evidence suggests that the pandemic has hit some gigs and side hustles – such as driving, babysitting, and housesitting – especially hard. Others, however, have boomed. Deliveries, surveys, cleaning, tutoring, dog walking, moving, home repairing, and remodeling – all of these, facilitated by websites that match gig workers and side hustlers with jobs, have grown. Overall, according to AppWork data, gig workers have suffered as have those who work in the conventional economy. This situation has, however, spurred many to innovate, to push their boundaries, to rethink their options. Etsy's revenues doubled in 2020 as new craftspeople joined and consumers spent significantly more (25–30%) on online retailers and service providers. In the third quarter of 2020, 10% of Etsy's revenue came from the sale of face masks.

Downsides to the gig economy also exist, of course. Rarely do gigs or side hustles offer health insurance or retirement benefits. Obamacare has relieved some but not all of the pressure on gig workers who worry about health insurance. Some are also concerned about the future of social security as it is subject to the vicissitudes of political winds. And, of course, the unexpected can upset all kinds of apple carts in unpredictable ways, especially those in the gig economy. Very few foresaw much less prepared for 9/11, the 2008 recession, or the Covid-19 pandemic. A related trend has been for businesses and higher education to hire temporary or contract employees for whom they don't have to pay benefits. The percentage of tenure-line faculty has decreased from 70% to 30% in the past few decades as salaries and benefits have increased. Adjuncts who constitute an increasing share of the higher education teaching force are lucky to make $7,500 per course even at well-funded institutions.

Of course, the internet creates opportunities for those adjuncts to become online college-level tutors. College tutors can charge upward of $50 an hour, meaning 5 hours of tutoring daily (25 students weekly) could generate as much income in 6 weeks as teaching a semester-long course with potentially dozens of students. Universities may soon have to raise adjuncts' salaries to compete for their time.

Gig work and side hustles afford people a high degree of self-determination and self-expression even as they demand diligence, flexibility, creativity, tolerance for uncertainty, and self-confidence. The trend that pre-dates the current pandemic suggests that the internet will continue to foster the growth of the gig economy and encourage people to take on side hustles. Pre-pandemic, a 2017 survey by Freelancers Union found that more than 50% of the US population would be freelancing by 2027. Freelancing is, in fact, expected to grow three times faster than other employment over the decade (Profeldt, 2017). The pandemic seems to have increased the appeal of independent workers: hiring managers report being 47% more inclined to hire independents than before the pandemic (Profeldt, 2020).

Once again, we face the question of how best to prepare students for a world in which the most satisfying and productive path may lead them, like Claire, to apply their talent and skills to temporary rather than long-term jobs. Freelancing continues to grow, in part, due to the pandemic but also due to its appeal to those who wish to exert control over their working lives and who are willing to forgo more money in exchange for flexibility, self-expression, and the satisfaction of exercising their talents and skills.

Knowledge Creation

Leaving Claire, cat on lap, in her study working on an illustration for a scientific presentation, we return to Brendan and his team as they go about their business on Discord. Earlier, in response to a need to make changes to a key program underlying the supply chain for production, the team had collaborated in determining the "shape of the program" so that team members have a shared idea of how they will collectively address the issue and ownership of the process. Rather than focusing solely on specific lines of codes, team members also have in mind what the final product will look like and what their colleagues will be doing. This encourages a flow of information and ideas among the team as they work and enables changes to the original design as challenges arise in coding.

This illustrates the nature of knowledge as a social product (Brown & Duguid, 2000). Certainly, individuals contribute to new knowledge but individuals are heirs to the ideas, knowledge, norms, language, beliefs, rituals, and artifacts that constitute cultures. Obama's observation that "none of us make it on our own" (a claim some found controversial) can be applied to knowledge. Even paradigm-shifting ideas such as Einstein's Theory of Relativity built on the ideas of Ernst Mach, Hendrik Lorentz, Michael Faraday, and many others who in their turn had been influenced by Newton and Copernicus – and so forth and so on. Newton famously observed that, "If I can see further, it's because I stand on the shoulders of giants." Although the shoulders on which we stand may not be those of giants, we all stand on the shoulders of those who came before us.

Recognition of the social nature of knowledge has grown over the past century or so and many organizations – like the one in which Brendan works – have sought to capitalize on this phenomenon. As noted above, the movement toward flatter organizations is due, in part, to the growing recognition that fewer administrative layers improve the flow of information and ideas. Transforming data into knowledge is a profoundly social enterprise (Brown & Duguid, 2000). Algorithms reflect our attempts to organize data in ways to collectively understand ourselves and our world. The legendary Douglas Engelbart, a pioneer in human–computer interaction, noted that "knowledge production is a group activity, not an individual one. Computers most radically and usefully extend our capabilities when they extend our ability to collaborate to solve problems beyond the compass of any single human mind" (Engelbart, 2003).

Unfortunately, this view of knowledge creation does not seem to inform the organization of learning in most schools. The unit of learning in typical education institutions remains the individual.

Learning is almost universally assessed individually, regardless of how learning may have been organized and occurred in classrooms and beyond. The grip that the concept of the individual student as the default "unit of learning" has on education was illustrated by the sad fate of Kentucky's ambitious attempt to include group tasks as part of the new assessments introduced as a keystone of the 1990 Kentucky Education Reform Act.

Overall, the assessments were remarkably progressive, requiring portfolios, responses to open-ended questions, and collaborative performance events. The latter acknowledged the social nature of knowledge development as well as the importance of collaborative skills. From the start, unfortunately, forces both within and outside of Kentucky opposed the assessment and the reforms more generally (Kannaple, et al., 1995). Opponents recognized that discrediting the assessments offered the quickest and easiest path to undermine other elements of the reform, especially curricular and instructional reforms. They arranged for psychometricians from Western Michigan University to review the assessments and testify before the Kentucky legislature. Using conventional psychometric standards that assume the individual student as the "unit of learning" to be assessed, they criticized the assessments for their lack of reliability and raised questions about their validity. The strategy worked for the opponents. Ultimately, conventional test items replaced the more ambitious parts of the assessments. In so doing, the critics achieved their goal of undermining the reforms more broadly. The inertia of the "grammar of schooling" is, as this example illustrates, truly formidable.

The default for assessing learning remains the individual student. International assessments such as PISA and TIMSS reinforce the commitment to measuring individual student knowledge and, until recently, ignored the collaborative ways in which knowledge is generated. Starting in 2015, PISA includes items intended to collect data on students' collaborative skills. On the 2015 version of the assessment, students interacted virtually with "classmates" to choose a response to a group chat addressing questions about a fictional country. Students also self-rated their collaborative skills as well as being rated by their teachers.

Given the outsized influence that PISA results have on educational policy globally, the inclusion of collaboration as a measured skill is promising, although we know little about how this has affected classroom activities. We do know that teachers teach what is tested so this may prompt educators to focus more on collaboration in classrooms. The danger is that the high-stakes nature of PISA in many contexts may lead educators to focus on how best to prepare students to score well on the collaboration task rather than redesign opportunities for students to collaborate on problem-solving and knowledge production.

The importance of collaborative skills is not limited to classrooms, of course. Most of the "big hairy problems" we face require a level of collaboration heretofore unseen. The good news is that technology enables a level of information sharing and collective knowledge creation previously unimaginable. As an example, Kevin Kelly, a founding editor of *Wired* and, earlier, the iconic *Whole Earth Catalog*, holds up Wikipedia as an example of collectivist knowledge creation (Kelly, 2017). Tens of thousands of "editors" create and populate entries of their devising. Over the decades, a cadre of self-appointed senior editors has emerged to oversee the operation, applying collectively developed criteria for data verification. Disputes over the validity of contributions are allowed in the expectation that time and the collective will eventually sort things out.

Similarly, open-source platforms such as Facebook, Mozilla Open Source Network, Linux, and Open Office depend on the collective of contributors to generate and test new ideas as well as products. As Kelly points out, however collective these platforms are, they all exhibit some form of organizational hierarchy required to function. Compared to the hierarchical characteristic of conventional businesses, these tend to be smaller and more flexible. This, Kelly argues, is a necessary complement to the openness of the process. However democratic, any collective criteria for verifying "truth claims" must exist and someone(s) has to monitor compliance with these criteria.

This growing, technology-enabled trend toward collectivist knowledge and solution creation is essential if we are to address a variety of other issues such as dramatic wealth and resource disparities, population migrations, pandemic threats, food and water insecurity, genetic engineering, and ocean conservation.

Organizational Culture and Norms

"Hey, sweetie, do you need me to pound your dough?" Brian asked his co-worker Hannah with a chuckle. Ignoring the question, Hannah continued shaping dough into sub-rolls to be baked in the ovens. Her fellow millennials at the wholesale bakery were not so tolerant. "Dude, stop being an asshole," said Jamie, looking up from the industrial-size mixer into which he was dumping flour and fixing his eyes on Brian. The five other millennials laboring in the production area had also stopped working and were staring at fiftyish Brian. Brian grinned sheepishly and responded, "Ok, ok – only kiddin' – we're cool." With that, he turned back to loading bread into the multi-shelved oven. Jamie glanced at Hannah, smiled sympathetically, and shook his head. "Just because you're new, you don't have to put up with that shit. If it happens again, let us know," he told her. Behind Jamie, his co-workers nodded in agreement before returning to their tasks.

This vignette illustrates one of the ways that organizational norms are changing and are likely to continue to do so. What is regarded as appropriate behavior is changing, albeit slowly in some organizations. Critics and some politicians sneer at what they label, "political correctness." This invective ignores the underlying shift in the experiences, attitudes, and perspectives of many younger workers. This isn't to say that sexism, racism, nativism, homophobia, ageism, and so forth will magically disappear in future organizations. Rather, these aggressions are much more likely to be called out, to be confronted, to be recognized for what they are than previously. A growing awareness means that injustices, aggression, and denigration due to gender, sexual identity, race, religion, and physical appearance or ability are more likely than ever to be called out and corrected. This is thanks, in part, to the internet – youth expectations for appropriate social and workplace behaviors have shifted and are likely to continue to change. Although injustice and prejudice will not disappear overnight, the ubiquity of social media and cell phones ensures that instances of biased actions are much more likely to be exposed more immediately and shared more widely than ever before. On one day alone – June 7, 2020 – YouTube registered over 100 million views of the George Floyd murder video.

A recent Pew survey revealed that millennials and Gen Xers appear to be significantly more tolerant of those who are different from themselves: more than 6 in 10 believe "increasing racial/ethnic diversity is good for society," a view shared by less than half of boomers and only 4 in 10 of the "silent" generation (Pew, 2019). Even among self-professed Republicans, twice as many millennials and Gen Xers believe that "blacks are treated less fairly than whites" than do boomers and members of the silent generation (4 in 10 vs. 2 in 10). Roughly half of millennials and Gen Xers believe gay and interracial marriages are "good for society" compared to a quarter or less of boomers and silent generation members. A majority of White young adults between the ages of 18 and 30 supported Black Lives Matter (BLM) protests this past summer. In short, the newer generations hold views that are more inclusive, tolerant, and cognizant of racial injustice than the generations before them.

Preparing Students for Future Organizations and Job Opportunities

As educators, changing workplaces and organizations raise several questions: How do we prepare students for organizations that are becoming more experimental and team oriented? How do we prepare students who may choose to become freelancers or entrepreneurs in the burgeoning gig economy? How do we prepare students for collaborative work and for contributing to collective knowledge creation? Logically, classroom opportunities to experience the value of collaborative work and diverse perspectives that result in new learning and understanding can help ready students for "team-based" organizations and collective knowledge creation.

Decades of evidence attest to the value of collaborative learning (Johnson & Johnson, 2009). In fact, cooperative learning has been called "an educational psychology success story." Over time, in some classrooms, learning activities have been organized increasingly around cooperative and collaborative groups. The question remains about how educators make use of these groups. Are these designed and orchestrated to cultivate the collaborative and other skills that future organizations will expect?

The key characteristics of productive collaborations are that the group members see the value of collaboration in their work and for the collaboration to be organized so members know their roles and responsibilities (Doğan & Adams, 2018; Zahedi et al., 2021). In a study of collaborative groups, Swedish students reported that "real group work" involves joint problem-solving that is a shared effort requiring the full group's competences (Chiriac & Granström, 2012). Some research suggests, however, that despite evidence of their efficacy, relatively few teachers regularly use collaborative groups. A 2017 study of over 200 Swiss teachers found that only a third regularly used collaborative groups whereas "the most frequent instructional strategies reported are traditional ones such as teacher-monitored, collective class discussion, transmission and individual work" (Buchs et al., 2017, p. 296).

Assuming that this and other related research paint a valid picture of classrooms, the question is: Why don't most teachers rethink how they organize students for learning and the tasks they assign? Researchers such as Buchs and colleagues (2017) found that teachers' beliefs about how students learn and their felt need to control the process, especially assessment, are major factors. Of equal or greater importance is the pressure teachers feel to "cover the curriculum" and the belief that collaboration takes too much time and effort.

High-stakes assessments and accountability policies loom over the curriculum, classroom organization, and learning tasks. As a result, many teachers worry that group work is an inefficient method for students to learn the knowledge needed to succeed on standardized tests. The consequences of poor results differentially affect students, teachers, families, and schools. The cost of poor performance for students from historically marginalized communities may be higher as good test scores may be one of the few ways they have to prove themselves and gain entry into the "culture of power" (Delpit, 1988). Schools with persistent low scores are subject to being closed or taken over by the state or a private school management organization. Little wonder that many educators are hesitant to adopt practices such as collaborative learning that may be viewed as inefficient. Better to focus on the information and skills needed to succeed on the standardized test.

As a result, most students do not have the opportunities to develop the self-management and collaborative skills that future-thinking organizations prize. For those students who choose to strike out on their own as freelancers or entrepreneurs, these skills may be of even greater value.

Evidence suggests that organizations, especially successful start-ups such as Brendan's, increasingly value independent and active learners who possess cognitive agility and flexibility. Successful organizations constantly monitor their environment, collecting and analyzing volumes of data to ensure they stay competitive and are fulfilling their mission. Many of these are team-based organizations that look for employees who show strong communication and collaborative skills, appreciation of diverse perspectives, team orientation, curiosity, resourcefulness, and trustworthiness. The latter is particularly important as team members need to know that their colleagues will carry out their assigned task professionally and in a timely manner. Where will these skills be cultivated?

As we have argued, our education systems remain top-down organizations, at the policy level as well as at the school and classroom levels. As many before us have noted, the system was designed to support an industrial world that valued compliance, standardization, and individual effort. The world that is evolving before our eyes is dramatically different. Top-down organizations are being challenged both by the nature of work that has become more team based and collaborative and by individuals who seek to forge their own paths. Whether they eventually work in organizations or pursue life as freelancers or entrepreneurs, students need more opportunities to develop their self-management and collaborative skills. They need opportunities to understand themselves as knowledge producers in collaboration with their colleagues and not merely as consumers of what others produce. The opportunities to make a living that have appeared over the past couple of decades foretell a future that places a premium on collaborative skills, initiative, and character, qualities that deserve a place in the curriculum alongside numeracy and literacy.

Summary

Technology is changing and will continue to change how and where we work. While school systems and schools remain hierarchical and students work largely individually, businesses are moving toward flatter structures that enable a freer flow of information and facilitate the work of teams. Businesses and non-profits increasingly search for workers who are effective communicators and collaborators and who appreciate the value of diverse perspectives. As globalization continues, the need for workers capable of working well with colleagues around the world will only grow.

The pandemic has also accelerated the movement to remote working and even as the virus recedes in many countries, remote and hybrid work appear to be here to stay. Zoom meetings are now commonplace for many employees. Evidence suggests that most workers are more productive if allowed to work from home at least part of each week. In addition, allowing employees to work remotely reduces overheads. Furthermore, when searching for new employees, many businesses need not limit the candidate pool to the immediate vicinity. Although time zone differences can be a limiting factor, candidates can be recruited and subsequently work from virtually anywhere. People with the skills needed to work well across cultures and to self-regulate will be at a premium.

Technology has also facilitated a growing number of entrepreneurial-minded people to work entirely outside conventional organizations. The internet has enabled a significant increase in freelancing, gig work, and side hustles. With little capital, people can sell their goods and services directly to customers. To take advantage of these opportunities requires not only a minimal knowledge of information and communications technology but other dispositions and skills as well. These include the ability to learn and adapt continually, to communicate clearly and persuasively, to persist in the face of adversity, and to empathize with and listen attentively to others unlike themselves.

Finally, the norms of behavior in organizations are changing, particularly in established organizations. Increasingly, businesses, as well as employees themselves, expect certain behaviors: respect for human diversity, cross-cultural awareness, appreciation for non-traditional families, ethical consciousness, and a team orientation. Although these may have been evident in some organizations previously, they are becoming increasingly prevalent norms.

The question is how our education system can prepare students for future organizations and the opportunities that technology affords for individual initiative.

References

Airtasker (2020, March 31). *The benefits of working from home*. Retrieved from: www.airtasker.com/blog/the-benefits-of-working-from-home/.

Brown, J., & Duguid, P. (2000). *The social life of information*. Cambridge, MA: Harvard Business Review Press.

Buchs, C., Filippoua, D., Pulfreyb, C., & Volpé, Y. (2017). Challenges for cooperative learning implementation: Reports from elementary school teachers. *Journal of Education for Teaching*, *43*(3), 296–306.

Chiriac, E. & Granström, K. (2012) Teachers' leadership and students' experience of group work, *Teachers and Teaching, 18*(3), 345–363, doi: 10.1080/13540602.2012.629842

Delpit, L. (1988). The silenced dialogue: Power and pedagogy in educating other people's children. *Harvard Educational Review*, *58*(3), 280–298.

Doğan, S., & Adams, A. (2018). Effect of professional learning communities on teachers and students: Reporting updated results and raising questions about research design. *School Effectiveness and School Improvement*, *29*(4), 1–26. doi: 10.1080/09243453.2018.1500921

Djankov, S., & Zhang, E. (2021). Startups boom in the United States during COVID-19. *Peterson Institute for International Economics*. Retrieved 03/02/2021 from: www.piie.com/blogs/realtime-economic-issues-watch/startups-boom-united-states-during-covid-19.

Engelbart, D. C. (2003, September 24). Improving our ability to improve: A call for investment in a new future. In *IBM Co-Evolution Symposium*, pp. 2–3. Retrieved 03/02/2021 from: www.dgsiegel.net/files/refs/Engelbart%20-%20Improving%20Our%20Ability%20to%20Improve:%20A%20Call%20for%20Investment%20in%20a%20New%20Future.pdf.

Johnson, D. W., & Johnson, R. T. (2009). An educational psychology success story: social Interdependence theory and learning. *Educational Researcher*, 38(5), 365–379. doi: 10.3102/0013189X09339057

Kannaple, P., Moore, B., Coe, P., & Aagaard, L. (1995). Opposition to Outcome-based Education in Kentucky. Paper presented at the Annual Meeting of the American Educational Research Association, San Francisco, CA. April 19, 1995. Retrieved from: www.academia.edu/29587274/Opposition_to_Outcome_Based_Education_in_Kentucky.

Kelly, K. (2017). *The inevitable: Understanding the 12 technological forces that will shape our future*. New York: Penguin.

Ozimek, A. (2020). Economist report: Future workforce. *Upwork*. Retrieved 03/02/2021 from: www.upwork.com/press/releases/economist-report-future-workforce.

Pew (2019). Americans see advantages and challenges in country's growing racial and ethnic diversity. Retrieved 03/02/21 from: www.pewresearch.org/social-trends/2019/05/08/americans-see-advantages-and-challenges-in-countrys-growing-racial-and-ethnic-diversity/.

Profeldt, E. (2017). Are we ready for a workforce that is 50% freelance? *Forbes*. Retrieved 03/01/2021 from: www.forbes.com/sites/elainepofeldt/2017/10/17/are-we-ready-for-a-workforce-that-is-50-freelance/?sh=5d1add513f82.

Profeldt, E. (2020). The coming boom for freelancer. *Forbes*. Retrieved 03/01/2021 from: www.forbes.com/sites/elainepofeldt/2020/06/12/the-coming-boom-for-freelancers/?sh=f6518475adc0.

Robison, J. (2020). Give up bossing, take up coaching: You'll like the results. *Gallup*. Retrieved 03/02/2021 from: www.gallup.com/workplace/282647/give-bossing-coaching-results.aspx.

Sweet, J. (2021, January–February). The loneliness pandemic. *Harvard Magazine*, *23*(3): 31–35.

Zahedi, S., Bryant, C. L., Iyer, A., & Jaffer, R. (2021). Professional learning communities at a primary and secondary school network in India. *Asia Pacific Education Review*. doi: 10.1007/s12564-020-09665-7

5

Pivot toward Skills Needed for the Present and Future

The world today is unquestionably different from the world 20 years ago and will be dramatically different in 20 years from today. Twenty years ago, we didn't have smartphones, driverless cars, thumb drives, Netflix, tablets, Alexa, Zoom, Facebook – among many other innovations. Technological changes have already profoundly transformed how we live, play, work, and educate. Changes in other areas have also contributed to the transformation of our lives. These include increasing political divisions, geopolitical conflicts, climate change, pandemics, and the arrival of new generations of citizens. Although we are uncertain about future changes, we are certain that the future will be thoroughly different. We are also certain that to not merely survive but also to thrive in the future, our children will need an education that differs significantly from that which students have experienced in the past.

This new education incorporates not only new pedagogies, new assessments, and new learning opportunities but also, and perhaps more important, new content. As we have argued, schools over the past century or more have taught mostly the same content: primarily literacy and numeracy augmented with a course in science and social studies as well as some arts, music, and physical education. Although these subjects remain relevant going forward, the question is: Are these legacy subjects adequate for an uncertain future that will certainly be shaped by yet-to-be-created technology as well as the challenges posed by climate change, inequalities, and geopolitical conflict?

DOI: 10.4324/9781315682884-6

Over the past couple of decades, a number of scholars and thought leaders have attempted to address this question, arguing forcefully for specific skills and knowledge.

21st-Century Skills

"21st-century skills" has become a popular phrase in education. Whether education leaders' and policymakers' ideas about 21st-century skills capture what is needed to thrive in this new age is open to question, yet the phrase is ubiquitous in discussions about what students will need to know and be able to do after leaving school.

Although several organizations and individuals have helped shape 21st-century skills, the Partnership for 21st-Century Skills was among the first to have a specific framework and the gravitas to popularize the idea. Founded as a non-profit in 2002, the founding partners included some of the biggest technological companies at the time, such as Dell, Apple, Microsoft, and Cisco, as well as non-profits such as the AOL Time Warner Foundation and the National Education Association. The US Department of Education also lent its support.

The partnership, which subsequently became the Partnership for 21st Century Learning, believes that "every child in America needs 21st century knowledge and skills to succeed as effective citizens, workers and leaders in the 21st century" (Partnership for 21st Century Skills, 2008). It worked to define and promote 21st-century skills as representing the skills, knowledge, and dispositions considered necessary for success in this century. According to the partnership, 21st-century skills include key skills in six areas: core subjects; 21st-century content; learning and thinking skills; information and communications technology (ICT) literacy; life skills; and 21st-century assessments.

More specifically, in its Framework for 21st Century Learning, the partnership describes "the skills, knowledge and expertise students should master to succeed in work and life in the 21st century" (Partnership for 21st Century Skills, 2007). They include:

- *Core subjects* (English, reading or language arts, world languages, arts, mathematics, economics, science, geography, history, government and civics) and *21st-century themes* (global awareness, financial, economic, business and entrepreneurial literacy, civic literacy, health literacy)
- *Learning and innovation skills* (creativity and innovation skills, critical thinking and problem-solving skills, communication and collaboration skills)
- *Information, media, and technology skills* (information literacy, media literacy, ICT literacy)
- *Life and career skills* (flexibility and adaptability, initiative and self-direction, social and cross-cultural skills, productivity and accountability, leadership and responsibility)

In their book, *21st Century Skills: Learning for Life in Our Times*, Bernie Trilling and Charles Fadel, two senior fellows at the partnership, further expanded the definition of 21st-century skills (Trilling & Fadel, 2009). They made a strong argument for the "seven Cs." The "seven Cs" are the essential skills for the 21st century: critical thinking and problem-solving; creativity and innovation; cross-cultural understanding; communications, information, and media literacy; computing and ICT literacy; career and learning self-reliance; and collaboration. Later, the partnership pared the "seven Cs" down to the "four Cs": collaboration, communication, critical thinking, and creativity. The "four Cs" have become widely disseminated and, it appears, education systems in some countries are attempting to incorporate them into their curricula (Care & Kim, 2018).

The Metiri Group developed a similar framework for the North Central Regional Education Lab in 2002. With the title *enGauge 21st Century Skills: Literacy in the Digital Age*, the framework is more specifically oriented to a future that is driven primarily by technology. This framework is said to be "based on two years of research" and "represents the fresh, serious, new perspective required in light of recent historical events, globalization, and the idiosyncrasies of the Digital Age" (Lemke, 2002, p.9). The Metiri Group proposes that the 21st century requires the following skills, knowledge, and dispositions:

- *Digital-Age Literacy* (Basic, scientific, economic, and technological literacies, visual and information literacies, multicultural literacy and global awareness)
- *Inventive Thinking* (Adaptability/managing complexity, self-direction, curiosity, creativity, and risk-taking, higher-order thinking and sound reasoning)
- *Effective Communication* (Teaming, collaboration, and interpersonal skills, personal, social, and civic responsibility, interactive communication)
- *High Productivity & Quality, State-of-the-Art Results* (Ability to prioritize, plan, and manage for results, effective use of real-world tools, the ability to create relevant, high-quality products)

(Lemke, 2002, p. 9)

The European Union has also attempted to define 21st-century skills, although they have used the term "key competences" rather than "skills." The European Parliament and the Council of the European Union have worked to "identify and define the key competences necessary for personal fulfillment, active citizenship, social cohesion and employability in a knowledge society." They arrived at eight key competences. Competences are "a combination of knowledge, skills and attitudes appropriate to the context" (The European Parliament & The Council of the European Union, 2006). The eight key competences are

(1) Communication in the mother tongue
(2) Communication in foreign languages
(3) Mathematical competence and basic competences in science and technology
(4) Digital competence
(5) Learning to learn
(6) Social and civic competences
(7) Sense of initiative and entrepreneurship
(8) Cultural awareness and expression

Additionally, "critical thinking, creativity, initiative, problem solving, risk assessment, decision taking, and constructive management of feelings" are considered important across all eight key competences.

R-Directed vs. L-Directed Skills

Daniel Pink's take on the skills and knowledge required in the 21st century also deserves attention. In his 2005 book, *A Whole New Mind: Moving from the Information Age to the Conceptual Age*, Pink contrasts two different categories of skills: L-directed thinking and R-directed thinking, meaning left brain directed and right brain directed. Although neuroscientists and brain researchers argue that many cognitive tasks draw on both hemispheres, Pink's proposal is, nonetheless, provocative. He suggests that L-directed thinking skills are sequential, literal, functional, textual, and analytic, functions that are typically assigned to the left hemisphere of the human brain. The R-directed thinking skills are characterized as simultaneous, metaphorical, aesthetic, contextual, and synthetic, typically functions assigned to the right hemisphere of the brain.

According to Pink, we have entered a new age, the 21st century, which makes R-directed skills more important than L-directed skills. He argues that three major factors, the three As – Asia, Automation, and Abundance – are the powers that made this transformation. In other words, technology, globalization, and the arrival of more leisure time and disposable income (at least for some) require skills most closely associated with the right hemisphere. Asia is a metaphorical reference to globalization which has enabled massive outsourcing and offshoring of manufacturing. The consequence is that many jobs that require the L-directed skills have been outsourced to Asia. Automation, resulting from technological developments, has led to many people being displaced, losing jobs that require the L-directed thinking skills. Abundance, the result of general economic growth in the developed world, has enabled people to consume more products and services that are produced by R-directed capabilities.

Pink asks people to consider their answers to three questions: Can someone overseas do it cheaper? Can a computer do it faster? Is what I am offering in demand in an age of abundance? Answers to these three questions can determine if their jobs will last. "If your answer to question 1 or 2 is yes, or if your answer to question 3 is no, you are in deep trouble," writes Pink because, "Mere survival today depends on being able to do something that overseas knowledge workers cannot do cheaper, that powerful computers can't do faster, and that satisfies the nonmaterial, transcendent desires of an abundant age" (Pink, 2005, p. 51). According to Pink, the ability to do something that cannot be outsourced or computerized or that satisfies the desires of the abundant age are the capabilities associated predominantly with the right hemisphere. Pink argues that:

> Today, the defining skills of the previous era – the "left brain" capabilities that powered the Information Age – are necessary but no longer sufficient. And the capabilities we once distained or thought frivolous – the "right brain" qualities of inventiveness, empathy, joyfulness, and meaning – increasingly will determine who flourishes and who flounders.
>
> (Pink, 2005, p. 3)

The R-directed skills that Pink thinks would be needed in the 21st century are

> *design*, the ability to "create something physically beautiful and emotionally transcendent"; *story*, the ability to "fashion a compelling narrative"; *symphony*, the ability to see "the big picture and be[ing] able to combine disparate pieces into an arresting new whole"; *empathy*, the ability to "understand what makes their fellow woman or man tick, to forge relationships, and to care for others"; *play*, the ability laugh and bring laughter to others; and *meaning*, the ability to "pursue more significant desires: purpose, transcendence, and spiritual fulfillment".
>
> (Pink, 2005, pp. 65–67)

Pink's list of abilities he believes critical for this century overlaps to some degree with the 21st-century skills and the Metiri Group's list of key competences. Yet, Pink seems to step back even further from immediate concerns to answer the critical question about which abilities sustain us but, somehow, are rarely considered by educational leaders and prognosticators. Arguably, *play* is as essential to our well-being as are healthy relationships and exercise. Similarly, nearly all of us seek *meaning* for our lives. We ask: Why am I here? What is my purpose? That these are absent from the various lists proposed for necessary skills and competences again raises the question: What is the purpose of education in an increasingly uncertain world?

Mindset, Grit, and Non-Cognitive Skills

Recently, a set of non-cognitive capabilities or dispositions has garnered much media attention and is touted as essential for the 21st century. Growth mindset is among them. Stanford psychologist Carol Dweck and colleagues' research findings support the significant impact that a growth mindset has on learning and other life outcomes (Dweck, 2006). According to Dweck and colleagues, human beings possess one of two types of mindsets: a growth mindset and a fixed mindset. Those with a growth mindset, that is, those who believe intelligence is malleable and can change, typically outperform those with a fixed mindset who tend to believe intelligence is inherent, predetermined, and unchangeable.

Similarly, "grit" has gained attention among educators and others in the past few years. The University of Pennsylvania psychology professor Angela Duckworth is among those who have popularized the idea. In her 2016 book, *Grit: The Power of Passion and Perseverance* (Duckworth, 2016), Duckworth argues that grit, a blend of passion and persistence, is key to success for everyone. Grit not only helps students to succeed academically but also helps others such as military cadets to succeed in training. Comparatively speaking, according to Duckworth, talent alone is no guarantee of success.

Other non-cognitive skills and traits have been touted as ingredients needed for success. Different people have used different names for these traits (Duckworth & Yeager, 2015; Wehmeyer & Zhao, 2020; Zhao et al., 2019). In general, they include emotional intelligence (Goleman, 1995), social intelligence (Zhao, 2016), entrepreneurial spirit (Zhao, 2012), self-awareness, curiosity, and resilience. Research has shown that academic achievement and cognitive skills alone do not predict success (Brunello & Schlotter, 2010; Levin, 2012).

Empirical Examination of 21st-Century Skills

A recent study took a different approach to 21st-century skills (Rios et al., 2020). Instead of theorizing about what is needed in the 21st century or testing the importance of a few traits or abilities, this group of researchers went through hundreds of thousands of job advertisements in search of critical 21st-century skills.

What they found may not necessarily be relevant in the future because the job advertisements were looking for employees today. Their results may also not address what the world actually needs because in this new world, many people do not work within the conventional employment scheme (Pink, 2002; Zhao, 2012). As noted in Chapter 4, many people work as entrepreneurs who create jobs and businesses or work as independent agents in the gig economy. Nonetheless, the study does give us a picture of what today's employers are looking for.

The researchers first conducted a literature review for 21st-century skills using terms such as "non-cognitive skills," "21st-century skills," "workplace skills," and "applied skills." The researchers found 16 articles of relevance. These articles included a list of skills: collaboration, problem-solving, communication skills, critical thinking, oral and written communication, ethics, cultural sensitivity, adaptability, creativity, continuous learning, self-direction, time management, professionalism, service orientation, leadership, and social intelligence.

The researchers then analyzed over 200,000 unique job advertisements for evidence of the 21st-century skills they identified. They found that of the roughly 142,000 analyzed advertisements, about 70% listed at least one of the identified 21st-century skills. At the same time, few job posts included more than two skills. The average number in each post was 1.62 and the maximum was 12. The most often-mentioned skills were oral communications, written communications, collaboration, and problem-solving. These skills appeared in 20% or more of the posts. Social intelligence and self-direction appeared in more than 10% of the job posts. The rest of the skills were included in fewer than 5% of the posts.

What Do We Need?

Many others have proposed qualities, skills, dispositions, and knowledge believed to be needed for the future (e.g., Barber et al., 2012; Wagner, 2008, 2012). These qualities, skills, dispositions, and knowledge can be called 21st-century skills or non-cognitive skills or personal traits (Duckworth & Yeager, 2015; Zhao et al., 2019). Whatever we call them does not really matter, but these proposed requirements are problematic in several ways.

The first problem is that these various proposed requirements are not defined in depth. Although these proposals have listed various skills, bodies of knowledge, and personal qualities and dispositions, they lack information on what would constitute competency or mastery. Various authorities have historically delineated what the various school subjects include with specific definitions of how much content should be included at different grade levels. Math, history, literacy, science, and other subjects have a prescribed scope and sequence. As a result, we know how much students are expected to learn in a given subject at a certain grade level. On the other hand, 21st-century skills and other similar listings lack such definitions. Thus, even though these proposals seem to define what students need to know, we have no idea how much they should know. For instance, we lack "benchmarks" for developing creativity, cultural competence, grit, growth mindset, valuing diversity, and so on. Without more detailed definitions, we lack guidance on helping students develop these skills and capacities. As educators, we don't know the right "dosage," to borrow a term from medicine, to reach competency or mastery.

The second problem is breadth. Besides a growth mindset and grit, the other proposals seem to suggest that all students need to master all the skills and knowledge as prescribed. These proposals include a wide range of skills and knowledge but the time for instruction remains the same as schools are currently structured. Is it actually possible for all students to master all the proposed skills, knowledge, and capacities?

As far back as the 1800s, the British philosopher Herbert Spencer was already pondering the question of what knowledge is of greatest worth, given the impossible amount of knowledge schools were expected to teach and students were expected to learn (Spencer, 1911). Today, educators are expected to teach an ever-increasing volume of subject-matter knowledge and newly created disciplines as well as the newly proposed skills, knowledge, and dispositions. Teaching the breadth of the proposed 21st-century skills to all students simply seems beyond the capacity of schools.

Third, the recommended new skills appear to ignore the reality of individual differences. For a multitude of nature and nurture reasons, students exhibit different cognitive strengths and weaknesses, interests, talents, and passions (Ridley, 2003; Zhao, 2018b). Conflicts arise from expecting that all students will learn the same material at the same pace when we know that individual students differ significantly in how, when, and how quickly they learn. They also differ in the degree and type of individual attention and direction needed to nurture their strengths and interests.

Acknowledging that all students cannot be expected to learn all the prescribed skills and knowledge in a predetermined time frame, we can dispense with attempts to force them to learn whatever is required on our schedule rather than their schedule. We can focus, instead, on supporting their learning when they are ready. This does not exclude the importance of all students learning ideas, information, and methods that are fundamental to their future learning and to their ability to participate, if they choose, in what has been called "the Great Conversation," especially as this conversation expands to include hitherto silenced or unheeded voices.

Fourth, there is the problem of conflicts among the outcomes of education. Already, we expect multiple educational outcomes. Adding 21st-century skills, or whatever body of new knowledge and skills, to what we already expect students to learn further complicates this issue. Learning time in schools is a zero-sum game. If we devote more time to certain subjects such as math and reading, students have less time to master other subjects such as science, social studies, and the arts. Yet, in many countries, expectations are for outcomes to be consistent across the subjects: that students should achieve mastery in all subject areas. An unanswered question remains: How will the inclusion of new skills and knowledge affect learning time for traditional subjects and expectations for outcomes? Given the strong relationship between time-on-task and learning, how will the scarce commodity that is learning time in school be allocated?

This highlights a potential tension between time and attention devoted to cognitive skills and to non-cognitive skills. For example, data from international assessments, the Programme for International Student Assessment (PISA) and Trends in

International Mathematics and Science Study (TIMSS), have shown that students' performance on cognitive test items correlate negatively with their confidence, valuation of the subjects, and interest in the subjects (Zhao, 2017, 2018c). Even a growth mindset does not always work well in all contexts. For instance, the 2020 PISA results show that in some education systems, mostly East Asia, a growth mindset has a negative correlation with PISA scores (Zhao, 2020). Thus, individual 21st-century skills and knowledge may, in fact, interact in unexpected and counterproductive ways. In some cases, they may actually be in conflict with each other.

Fifth, although one or two individual traits or skills may be particularly important for success in life or academics, such traits or skills are highly unlikely to work for all people in every context. A growth mindset may work for some students or people in some contexts or perhaps work for all the sampled individuals in vitro. But it is impossible that it works to make people successful in real life in all contexts. The case of the negative correlation between PISA scores and a growth mindset among Chinese students is a great example. The same is true for grit. A synthesis of the research has found it to be much less powerful than advertised (Ivcevic & Brackett, 2014). Thus, we must consider what matters in which contexts and for whom.

Finally, economic success has been offered as a primary justification for these 21st-century skills. But, of course, education is for much more than economic success alone. As discussed earlier in this book, human beings are entering a different world of work, living, play, and education. This new world requires not only skilled workers but also citizens who can think rationally and collaborate successfully, who are critical consumers of information and data, who are skeptics of simplistic explanations of and solutions to complex problems, who are comfortable with different cultures, and who are prepared to participate in and enjoy the products of creativity in all their manifestations. They are also able to spend their leisure time in fulfilling pursuits and continue learning across their lifetime, taking advantage of a range of resources that include online communities. The skills and knowledge to support living, creating, playing, and learning in the new world may or may not be the same as those needed for working.

Creative, Entrepreneurial, and Unique

To address these issues requires a different approach to thinking about how best to prepare our children to thrive amid the uncertainties of a technologically transformed world. The phrase "21st-century skills" seems less apt as we are already more than two decades into the 21st century. A number of people object to the phrase because many of these cognitive and non-cognitive skills, knowledge, and dispositions were also relevant in past centuries. Although this is true, access to opportunities to learn these skills was largely limited to elites. Schools to which most people had access did not emphasize them (Zhao, 2012, 2018b). Seminars of 12 or 13 well-nourished students discussing character development in *Crime and Punishment* or string theory – an imaginable scenario in elite private schools – were rarely found in public schools across the world.

The new approach to increasing access to powerful knowledge and skills is to shift away from treating all students the same and expecting skills to be mastered by all students at the same level and in the same time frame. Schools have long imposed pre-set curricula on students, regardless of their readiness for or interest in the material. Moreover, schools also assume that students' age is the most relevant factor in deciding the knowledge and skills they should learn. If students are of the same age, typically they are grouped together, they attend the same class, they are taught the same content in the same ways, and they take the same exams. This ignores what we know about the variability of the cognitive and social development of children and youth (Ashiabi & O'Neal, 2015; De Ribaupierre & Lecerf, 2018; Nesselraode, 1991). Although schools have been able to argue that personalizing learning experiences is beyond the resources available, technology has made this contention mute. Current technologies enable a previously unavailable level of personalization – and we can anticipate that new and evolving technologies will allow us to tailor, even more effectively, learning opportunities to the needs, interests, schedule, and capacities of each student (Craig, 2021).

The new approach takes students as unique individual human beings who are, inherently, learners. They are diverse individuals, each with a unique mix of talents, passions, skills, experiences, abilities, strengths, and weaknesses. They develop and dwell in different places and cultures. Their uniqueness is not merely a characteristic; it is a potential resource. Cultivating and developing this resource are key to germinating the innovations and problem solutions needed for the uncertain future that awaits us (Zhao, 2009, 2012, 2018b).

A Common Body of Knowledge, Skills, and Dispositions

Even as education is tailored to individual students, the cultivation of individual uniqueness requires a foundation of common skills, dispositions, and knowledge that is critical for any society and what past generations termed "worthy home and community membership." These commonalities enable individuals to work, live, and perform civic duties together. These skills, dispositions, and knowledge can be decided by governments or other authorities but, at a minimum, should include global awareness and competence, digital literacy, civic values and responsibilities, and basic literacy and numeracy. These fundamental skills, dispositions, and knowledge should take up, perhaps, 30% of the school curriculum (Zhao, 2021).

Needed is a step back from the current subject-matter curricula of schools. The question of what is worth knowing requires input from a wide swathe of people, not just policymakers, disciplinary communities, and educators. Some years ago, Murnane and Levy (1996) surveyed employers about the skills needed to be productive workers in their enterprises. What they learned is that the expectations are, relative to current curriculum standards, modest:

> (1) the ability to read at the ninth-grade level or higher; (2) the ability to do math at the ninth-grade level or higher; (3) the ability to solve semi-structured problems where hypotheses must be tested; (4) the ability to work in groups with persons of different backgrounds; (5) the ability to communicate effectively, both orally and in writing; and (6) the ability to use computers to carry out simple tasks.
>
> (Murnane & Levy, 1996)

The specific recommendations are less important than their manageability. These seem within the grasp of all high school students and the capacities of schools and leave room for the additional cognitive and non-cognitive skills and knowledge we describe below.

The assumption among those who create pre-K to Grade 12 curriculum standards is that all the knowledge and skills they believe incumbent upon them to help students develop must be learned in the space of 12 or more years of formal schooling. Given the affordances of technology, which will only increase in the future, this assumption no longer applies. If students wish to pursue a subject matter beyond the fundamentals, if they want to learn calculus, organic chemistry, African-American history, 19th-century Russian novels, Mandarin, and so on, the internet offers not only multiple online resources but also individual tutoring sessions, some of which are free. We can let go of the assumption that educators are obliged to ensure students master the multitudinous information, ideas, and skills that are usually crammed into curriculum standards and outlines. Rather, we can focus more on helping students learn on their own: how they can do historical research, scientific inquiry, literary analysis, statistical analysis, and so on. We can help them connect to communities of inquiry in which members teach one another and collaborate on research. These suggestions are predicated on students learning to question and investigate truth claims, as we discuss in Chapter 1.

We can also help them determine how well they understand whatever they study and develop the metacognitive skills critical for successful learning. Awareness of the Dunning–Kruger Effect is a starting point. Based on their research, Dunning and Kruger found that we have a tendency to overestimate our knowledge, understanding, and skills (Dunning & Kruger, 1999). The lower our performance on tasks, the more likely we are to judge our performance positively. For many of us, the less we know about a topic, the more we may believe we know. This offers an example of how the non-cognitive disposition of self-awareness intersects with our cognitive behaviors and development.

The evidence suggests that not only can students learn to monitor their own mastery but also that learning to do so significantly enhances their learning (Black & Wiliam, 1998). In school-based experiments, students of teachers trained in cultivating self-assessment and self-monitoring consistently outperform their peers whose teachers lack such training (Panadero et al., 2017). Equipped with the skills to monitor their own learning, discipline-specific methods of inquiry, and basic knowledge of key information, processes, and ideas in the traditional subject matters, students can truly become the much-touted "lifelong learners" who are featured in 21st-century skills literature.

Local Knowledge

Students grow up in various local cultures. Deep connections with the history, values, and traditions of local communities imbue individuals with senses of self-worth, responsibility, and identity. An Alaska Native leader, Harold Napoleon, once urged a graduating class at a rural Native high school:

> The day will come when some Alaska Native will have blue eyes and blond hair. What makes us Natives is not our blood but the respect for our way of life, history and traditions. We know who we are. This is what matters.
>
> (Personal communication, 1981)

A strong sense of identity, of one's roots, can foster acceptance and respect for others who are products of starkly different cultures, dispositions needed to succeed in a global society.

Every school or school district is unique with its own history. It is shaped by the values of the local culture and community. Schools owe it to their communities to create opportunities for students to learn about the communities, their history, values, and traditions. In some places in the United States and elsewhere, these histories include racism and other forms of discrimination as well as violence. As unpleasant as this information is, it is part of the collective legacies of communities and deserves a place alongside the values, people, traditions, and accomplishments that have sustained communities.

The importance of local knowledge to students' sense of identity and responsibility suggests that 20–30% of the curriculum should be devoted to the study of local values, history, and traditions. Because some communities also harbor prejudices toward others, often those with whom they have little or no direct interactions, the significance of the 21st-century skills that focus on appreciating and valuing diversity is all the more important. Recognizing that no group can claim exclusive rights to truth, that others may have knowledge and perspectives critical to addressing problems we face collectively, is a key element in global literacy. Local knowledge and the proposed 21st-century skills are complementary not antithetical. Just as self-awareness of one's own learning and the limits of one's knowledge are essential for learning, so too are the social, historical, and cultural roots of our beliefs, attitudes, and opinions.

Self-Determined Knowledge

This leaves 40% of school time for students to develop their individual interests and abilities. Every student has his or her own natural-born talent, passions, and desires (Gardner, 1983, 2006; John et al., 2008; Reiss, 2000, 2004; Zhao, 2018a, 2018b). Instead of forcing students to give up their own strengths and passions with a one-size-fits-all curriculum, assessment, pedagogy, and organization, schools should move toward a strength-based education. Schools should work with students and parents to help develop a personalized education plan for every student. A model for this has been in front of educators for decades: individual education plans (IEP) required for each student with special needs. The involvement of parents in developing, implementing, and monitoring the IEP demonstrates the vital role that parents can and should play.

The personalized learning plan is a roadmap to enable students to develop their strengths, address their weaknesses, and cultivate their passions. They can take courses or create their own learning courses from various online resources. They can learn from experts, teachers, and classmates. Equally important, they can participate in online learning communities and interact with experts and peers from around the world. The overall purpose is for each student to take ownership of their learning and develop a unique "jagged profile of abilities."

"A jagged profile of abilities" (Rose, 2016) acknowledges that each person has strengths in some areas and weaknesses in others. No one is expected to master every skill and body of knowledge at the same level or at the same time or speed. As we argue above, everyone is expected to master certain prescribed skills and knowledge at a basic level and everyone will also identify specific fields and specialties in which they hope to excel.

When each person develops a unique jagged profile, he or she needs to develop their creativity and entrepreneurial spirit (Zhao, 2012). Creativity and entrepreneurial spirit are both, arguably, inherent human qualities (Sawyer, 2012). Human beings rely on creativity and entrepreneurial spirit to survive. Human learning is, at base, a process of creation. As we are exposed to new experiences, we constantly construct or create hypotheses about the world based on prior experiences and then test these hypotheses. We do not simply remember what we learned from others. We must actively create our own understandings of the world. Likewise, entrepreneurially spirited human beings scan their environments seeking opportunities and then set about attempting to create something valuable for themselves and others. They typically regard setbacks and failures as learning opportunities. The failure rate for startups is very high yet the entrepreneurial spirit drives many who have failed to try again, and again, and again.

Creativity and entrepreneurial spirit need to be fostered as human beings grow up. That we have the natural ability to create and the natural tendency to be entrepreneurial does not mean that these are sufficient for us to thrive in the new world. Scholars have identified four levels of creativity (Kaufman & Beghetto, 2009): mini c, little c, pro c, and big c. "Mini c" is natural and inherent in learning of which everyone is capable. "Little c," the next level, requires support and feedback from others to create something that is valuable to others. "Pro c" creativity is the ability to create at a professional level and in a professional venue. This level requires deliberate practice and training in a certain profession to produce results of professional value. "Big c" creativity is transformational and exceptional. Not everyone, even with training and practice, can achieve this level of creativity. Using these levels as a guide, all students should receive the support needed to reach at least the pro c level. This level of creativity requires practice and deep knowledge in specific domains.

The entrepreneurial spirit involves creating value for others. Entrepreneurs are not only those who start or manage businesses that create value for customers, but they are also those who operate in the non-profit world. They are social entrepreneurs who create social values for others. This may be through financially self-sustaining means (Dees, 1998; Martin & Osberg, 2007) or through public services (Harris & Kinney, 2004). In addition, intrapreneurs create value for others operating within existing organizations (Swearingen, 2008; Zhao, 2012).

Through creativity and entrepreneurial spirit, we translate our unique abilities into services and products of value to others. When each person's unique strengths and passions produce something valuable to others, he or she becomes valuable, even indispensable. When people create value for others, rather than looking for jobs, they are creating jobs.

Creating jobs is perhaps one of the most important activities in the future world. People who can't find a job and receive a government-guaranteed income will need to find meaningful ways to spend their time. Creating value for others, for the community, and for the world gives these people meaningful and productive things to do. As machines will increasingly take over most of the manual and repetitive work, displaced workers will need to have creative and entrepreneurial skills as well as a belief in their capacity for creativity and innovation. They will need to identify problems and needs that smart machines cannot address and create solutions and fill needs.

Creating value and services with one's unique abilities and passions is also a way to stay happy. Humanistic psychologist Abraham Maslow's concepts of self-actualization and self-transcendence (Maslow, 1954, 1973, 1996) point out the need for human beings to realize their potential and the need to create value for others and the broad world. Positive psychologist Martin Seligman says authentic happiness comes from using "your signature strengths and virtues in the service of something much larger than you are" (Seligman, 2002, p. 263). With the decline of available conventional jobs, people will need to use their initiative and creativity to craft productive activities that give purpose, meaning, and even joy to their lives.

Summary

There is little doubt that the world in the future, the near future, will be different from today and definitely different from yesterday. Equally certain is that the future is unpredictable. We are not entirely sure what the future will look like. That machines will replace humans, especially in activities informed by L-directed thinking, is almost certain. Evolving technology will bring many traditional industries to an end and also promises the creation of new enterprises. Globalization is likely to continue apace, intruding further into the lives of everyone unless, of course, geopolitics and climate change generate debilitating levels of chaos.

The world will be increasingly online as well. More commerce and business will be conducted online. The potential for an improving world or an increasingly chaotic one seems equally possible. We may confront a world with too few jobs and engage in an ongoing battle with technology for new jobs. We may continue to huddle with our respective tribes and yet be drawn into larger communities. We may be dealing with warring factions and divided societies and yet be involved in creating new communities of our own. Fake news will continue to exist alongside real news.

Living in this uncertain world requires new skills and knowledge, both cognitive and non-cognitive. To lead the uncertain future into a better future for all human beings requires not only new skills and knowledge but also attention to ethics and morality. In this chapter, we have reviewed different proposals for new skills, knowledge, and dispositions for the future. We have also made the argument for reassessing our historical habit of imposing the same body of skills and knowledge on all children. We argue that it is individuals and individuals within vibrant communities who develop the strengths and pursue the passions that will succeed in the future. Fueling success will be creativity and entrepreneurial spirit to serve others. Cultivating and developing these qualities should be a primary purpose of education.

Ultimately, to avoid potential catastrophes and move the world in the direction of valuing and sustaining all of us requires, at a minimum: ethical and moral character; a critical mindset and tools to learn across the lifespan; an understanding of others and an appreciation of diversity; and the talent, skills, knowledge, and dispositions to take advantage of new technologies, to make good use of globalization, and to unite with others to create a better future. A "better future" includes peace and prosperity for all of us, not just the privileged.

References

Ashiabi, G. S., & O'Neal, K. K. (2015). Child social development in context: An examination of some propositions in Bronfenbrenner's bioecological theory. *SAGE Open*. https://doi.org/10.1177/2158244015590840.

Barber, M., Donnelly, K., & Rizvi, S. (2012). *Oceans of Innovation: The Atlantic, The Pacific, Global Leadership and the Future of Education*. Retrieved from: www.ippr.org/publications/oceans-of-innovation-the-atlantic-the-pacific-global-leadership-and-the-future-of-education.

Black, P., & Wiliam, D. (1998). Assessment and classroom learning. *Assessment in Education*, *5*(1), 7–74.

Brunello, G., & Schlotter, M. (2010). *The effect of non cognitive skills and personality traits on labour market outcomes*. Retrieved from: www.epis.pt/downloads/dest_15_10_2010.pdf.

Care, E., & Kim, H. (2018). Assessment of 21st century skills: The issue of authenticity. In E. Care, P. Griffin & M. Wilson (Eds.) *Assessment and teaching of 21st century skills: Research and applications*. Cham: Springer.

Craig, S. (2021, February 23). A.I. here, there, and everywhere. *The New York Times*. Retrieved from: www.nytimes.com/2021/02/23/technology/ai-innovation-privacy-seniors-education.html?surface=home-discovery-vi-prg&fellback=false&req_id=345367706&algo=identity&variant=no-exp&imp_id=854343319&action=click&module=Science%20%20Technology&pgtype=Homepage.

De Ribaupierre, A., & Lecerf, T. (2018). On the importance of intraindividual variability in cognitive development. *Journal of Intelligence*, 6(2), 17. https://doi.org/10.3390/jintelligence6020017

Dees, J. G. (1998). The meaning of "Social Entrepreneurship." Retrieved from: www.caseatduke.org/documents/dees_sedef.pdf.

Duckworth, A. (2016). *Grit: The power of passion and perseverance*. New York: Scribner.

Duckworth, A. L., & Yeager, D. S. (2015). Measurement matters: Assessing personal qualities other than cognitive ability for educational purposes. *Educational Researcher*, *44*(4), 237–251.

Dweck, C. S. (2006). *Mindset: The new psychology of success* (1st ed.). New York: Random House.

Gardner, H. (1983). *Frames of mind: The theory of multiple intelligences*. New York: Basic Books.

Gardner, H. E. (2006). *Multiple intelligences: New horizons in theory and practice*. New York: Basic Books.

Goleman, D. (1995). *Emotional intelligence*. New York: Bantam Books.

Harris, M., & Kinney, R. (Eds.) (2004). *Innovation and entrepreneurship in state and local government*. Lanham, MA: Lexington Books.

Ivcevic, Z., & Brackett, M. (2014). Predicting school success: Comparing conscientiousness, grit, and emotion regulation ability. *Journal of Research in Personality*, *52*, 29–36.

John, O. P., Robins, R. W., & Pervin, L. A. (2008). *Handbook of personality: Theory and research* (3rd ed.). New York: Guilford Press.

Kaufman, J. C., & Beghetto, R. A. (2009). Beyond big and little: The four C model of creativity. *Review of General Psychology*, *13*(1), 1–12.

Kruger, J., & Dunning, D. (1999). Unskilled and unaware of it: How difficulties in recognizing one's own incompetence lead to inflated self-assessments. *Journal of Personality and Social Psychology*, *77*(6): 1121–1134. doi: 10.1037/0022-3514.77.6.1121

Lemke, C. (2002). *NCREL's enGauge 21st century skills: digital literacies for a digital age*. Napier, IL: NCREL.

Levin, H. M. (2012). More than just test scores. *Prospects: The Quarterly Review of Comparative Education*, *42*(3), 269–284.

Martin, R. L., & Osberg, S. (2007). Social entrepreneurship: The case for definition. *Stanford Social Innovation Review*, 2007 (spring), 29–39. Retrieved from: www.skollfoundation.org/wp-content/uploads/2010/09/2007SP_feature_martinosberg.pdf.

Maslow, A. H. (1954). *Motivation and personality* (1st ed.). New York: Harper.

Maslow, A. H. (1973). *Fragment of an unfinished book, circa 1970. Cited in R Lowry, A.H. Maslow: An intellectual portrait*. Monterey, CA: Brooks/Cole.

Maslow, A. H. (1996). Critique of self-actualization theory. In E. Hoffman (Ed.) *Future visions: The unpublished papers of Abraham Maslow* (pp. 26–32). Thousand Oaks, CA: Sage.

Murnane, R. J., & Levy, F. (1996). *Teaching the new basic skills: Principles for educating children to thrive in a changing economy*. New York: Martin Kessler Books, Free Press.

Nesselraode, J. (1991). The warp and the woof of the developmental fabric. In R. Downs, L. Liben, & D. Palermo (Eds.) *Visions of aesthetics, the environment and development: The legacy of Joachim F. Wohlwill*. Hillsdale, NJ: Erlbaum.

Panadero, E., Jonsson, A., & Botella, J. (2017). Effects of self-assessment on self-regulated learning and self-efficacy: Four meta-analyses. *Educational Research Review*, 22, 74–98.

Pink, D. H. (2002). *Free agent nation: The future of working for yourself*. New York: Warner Books.

Pink, D. (2005). *A whole new mind: moving from the information age to the conceptual age*. New York, NY: Riverhead Books.
Reiss, S. (2000). *Who am I?: The 16 basic desires that motivate our behavior and define our personality*. New York: Jeremy P. Tarcher/Putnam.
Reiss, S. (2004). Multifaceted nature of intrinsic motivation: The theory of 16 basic desires. *Review of General Psychology*, *8*(3), 179–183. Retrieved from: http://sitemaker.umich.edu/cognition.and.environment/files/reiss-intrinsic-mot.pdf.
Ridley, M. (2003). *Nature via nurture: Genes, experience, and what makes us human* (1st ed.). New York: HarperCollins.
Rios, J. A., Ling, G., Pugh, R., Becker, D., & Bacall, A. (2020). Identifying critical 21st-century skills for workplace success: A content analysis of job advertisements. *Educational Researcher*, *49*(2), 80–89.
Rose, T. (2016). *The end of average: How we succeed in a world that values sameness* (1st ed.). New York: HarperOne.
Sawyer, K. (2012). *Explaining creativity: The science of human innovation.* Oxford: Oxford Press.
Seligman, M. E. P. (2002). *Authentic happiness: Using the new positive psychology to realize your potential for lasting fulfillment*. New York: Free Press.
Spencer, H. (1911). What knowledge is of most worth. In H. Spencer (Ed.), *Essays on education and kindred subjects*. London: Dent/Aldine Press.
Swearingen, J. (2008, April 10). Great intrapreneurs in business history. Retrieved from: www.cbsnews.com/8301-505125_162-51196888/great-intrapreneurs-in-business-history/.
Trilling, B., & Fadel, C. (2009). *21st century skills: Learning for life in our times.* San Francisco, CA: John Wiley & Sons.
Wagner, T. (2008). *The global achievement gap: Why even our best schools don't teach the new survival skills our children need – And what we can do about it.* New York: Basic Books.
Wagner, T. (2012). *Creating innovators: The making of young people who will change the world.* New York: Scribner.
Wehmeyer, M., & Zhao, Y. (2020). *Teaching students to become self-determined learners*. Alexandria, VA: ASCD.
Zhao, Y. (2009). *Catching up or leading the way: American education in the age of globalization*. Alexandria, VA: ASCD.
Zhao, Y. (2012). *World class learners: Educating creative and entrepreneurial students*. Thousand Oaks, CA: Corwin.
Zhao, Y. (2016). *Counting what counts: Reframing education outcomes.* Bloomington, IN: Solution Tree Press.
Zhao, Y. (2017). What works can hurt: Side effects in education. *Journal of Educational Change*, *18*(1), 1–19.
Zhao, Y. (2018a). Personalizable education for greatness. *Kappa Delta Pi Record*, *54*(3), 109–115.

Zhao, Y. (2018b). *Reach for greatness: Personalizable education for all children*. Thousand Oaks, CA: Corwin.

Zhao, Y. (2018c). *What works may hurt: Side effects in education*. New York: Teachers College Press.

Zhao, Y. (2020, January 4). PISA Peculiarities (1): Why doesn't growth mindset work for Chinese students? Retrieved from: http://zhaolearning.com/2020/01/04/pisa-peculiarities-1-why-doesnt-growth-mindset-work-for-chinese-students/.

Zhao, Y. (2021). *Learners without borders*. Thousand Oaks, CA: Corwin.

Zhao, Y., Wehmeyer, M., Basham, J., & Hansen, D. (2019). Tackling the wicked problem of measuring what matters: Framing the questions. *ECNU Review of Education*, *2*(3), 262–278.

6

Technology to the Rescue

How Education Can Use Technology to Achieve a Better Future

Technological changes have been a major force in driving educational changes (Goldin & Katz, 2008), and they are also one of the most important factors in helping education meet the needs of a changing society (Zhao et al., 2015). The first and second industrial revolutions led to massive shifts in society and also created the modern education system, which helped build a workforce for the industrialized society. Today, as human society enters the Fourth Industrial Revolution and the many uncertainties created by new geopolitics, political divisions, globalization, and online platforms, the current education system is no longer sufficient to help our children thrive in the new world. The call for a new education system has been getting louder in recent years (Dintersmith, 2018; Pink, 2006; Wagner, 2008, 2012; Zhao, 2012). Technology plays a significant role in inventing and delivering this new education (Zhao, 2021; Zhao et al., 2015).

For more than 100 years, the role of modern electronic technology in improving education has been discussed and tested in various ways. In 1923, Thomas Edison predicted that the film projector he invented would soon replace teachers (The Associated Press, 1923). In the subsequent years, every major technological invention has been experimented with for educational purposes. Film, radio, and TV have been used to convey high-quality educational experiences to millions of students (Cuban, 1986). Computers, especially personal computers, have been eagerly placed in education to teach computer skills and support new forms of learning. Of course, the internet and all sorts of associated technologies have been used to enhance education.

DOI: 10.4324/9781315682884-7

The idea that technology has tremendous power to improve and transform education is deeply rooted in the minds of many technologists and educators.

However, despite the potential power of technology to support the transformation of education, it was not until the massively damaging event of the Covid-19 pandemic that educators had a chance to experience it. Starting in January 2020, the virus began to spread across the world, forcing millions of schools to close for at least a short period of time with some schools having to close more than once. Over 96% of the world's students lost access to their physical schools for a period of time (UNICEF, 2020).

When schools were closed, remote learning was offered. The change was fast and everyone was unprepared. Most teachers had not prepared to teach online or were not trained to teach online. Despite the growth of online education prior to Covid-19, the majority of formal schooling operates in the physical world, where teachers meet and teach students in the classroom inside a school. But the Covid-19 pandemic changed everything. In essence, it forced millions of teachers to teach online and billions of students to learn remotely.

As a result, almost all teachers and students have had an experience with technology in education. The experiences have been diverse. Different countries and schools implemented remote learning in different ways. Some did TV broadcasting of lessons combined with online teacher tutoring. Some allowed students to do project-based learning, enabling students to pursue their own interests. Some replicated in-person classrooms, essentially offering online what would have been offered in the classroom.

The different models of remote learning produced different outcomes. Some practices may have been better than others. However, whatever the model or consequence, technology played a vital role in keeping education going for students. Without technology, it is difficult to imagine what could have been done to offer students access to education when schools were closed. The last massive pandemic, the Spanish Flu, occurred about 100 years ago. While it was as consequential as the Covid-19 pandemic, there were not as many schools around the world and it was likely that remote learning was not an option for the majority of students.

With the recognition of the role of technology in enabling continuing education remotely when schools were closed and the various experiences teachers and students had with technology during the Covid-19 pandemic, we should also keep in mind that the power of technology to improve education is much more than translating courses to online or simply offering students an educational experience when schools are unable to do so. Furthermore, it is important to understand that technology can play a much more significant role in transforming education. It is thus essential for schools and educators not to abandon their technology uses when schools reopen. Instead, they should continue their efforts and explore the full range of contributions that technology can make in creating a new education system in the Fourth Industrial Revolution.

Technology and Teachers

Before we discuss the potential roles of technology in education, we need to dispel some of the fantasies that technology enthusiasts have promoted and are still promoting because such fantasies are at best wishful thinking and at worst harmful to education. These fantasies have been in existence for a long time and have often stimulated unrealistic enthusiasm and unnecessary anxiety in education. They often failed to be actualized because they could not be realized. However, because technology changes fast, when one fantasy is proven to be unrealistic, another one quickly pops up. This is why education has never been short of fantasies driven by technology.

One of the most widely held fantasies is that technology can replace human teachers. Thomas Edison was not alone in thinking that films could record the teaching of a few excellent teachers and then reach millions of students so that teachers were not needed for small groups of students in schools. Promoters of radio and TV technologies had similar fantasies (Cuban, 1986). They believed that the teaching of a group of wonderful teachers could be broadcast to students so that they did not need teachers locally. Anyone who had access to radio and TV could learn from the broadcast. Because of the reach of radio and TV, this anyone was essentially everyone. While radio and TV universities were established in various locations, ultimately teachers were not replaced and schools continued to operate the way they used to.

Technology advances. New technological revolutions continue to give people hope that teachers can be replaced, and schools can be shut down. The internet, which came of age in the 1990s, created new fantasies for people who might have been disappointed with the results of radios and TVs in education. In 1992, when the internet was just about to explode into a revolution, Lewis Perleman wrote the book, *School's Out: Hyperlearning, the New Technology, and the End of Education* (Perelman, 1992). In the book, Perelman makes the argument that technology enables the possibility of parental choice of schools and student choice of programs and, more importantly, new forms of learning, without teachers and schools, are possible. It's almost 30 years since Perelman's book and schools remain unchanged. Teachers are still integral to and essential in schools.

Online education has given the enthusiast another hope to replace teachers with technological solutions. The internet has enabled many education institutions and individuals to create and offer online education. In fact, the growth of online programs in education went way beyond what Perelman imagined. Clayton Christensen and colleagues' book *Disrupting Class: How Disruptive Innovation Will Change the Way the World Learns* (Christensen et al., 2010) and associated works in education provided new models of education that would change education dramatically. But the world of education remains the same. The various online programs, YouTube videos, Khan Academy, and massive open online courses (MOOCs) did not bring the transformation that would radically change the role that teachers play in schools.

Will teachers be replaced by technology? Can teachers be replaced by technology? These are very tough questions. But for now and in the foreseeable future, the answer is no. There are several reasons why technology will not and cannot replace teachers in schools, at least for now.

The first reason is, of course, tradition or the grammar of schooling (Tyack & Tobin, 1994). Schools have a perpetual image in the mind of the public and educators. They should have time bells to indicate when classes start and end. They should have knowledge splintered into subjects. They should have students grouped into different classes and each of them managed and taught by an adult teacher. This grammar of schooling has been in existence since schools started and it represents how schools should operate (Zhao, 2020). Over the past 100 years, many meaningful efforts have been put forward to undo the grammar of schooling but with very little success. Technology may be powerful but not powerful enough to transform schools out of the grammar of schooling. Thus, as a result, when technology meets teachers, teachers win (Cuban, 1986, 2001).

The second reason is that learning is fundamentally social (Bransford et al., 2000; National Academies of Sciences & Medicine, 2018). Individual students can and certainly do learn on their own from reading, listening, and watching materials without necessarily the instruction of a teacher in front of them (Mitra, 2012, 2019). In fact, we all learn through reading books, watching news, and listening to podcasts. But these individual acts of learning can only be part of our education because both the content and outcome can be very limited.

A bigger part of learning is through socially interacting and working together with other people and peers. Human beings devote 10–12 years educating their young and those 10–12 years cannot be just watching YouTube videos or interacting with computer software. Instead, the 10–12 years are an organized journey of community-based learning activities that include many opportunities for human interactions. The organization needs to be done by teachers or other prepared adults.

The third reason is that education is much more than the instruction of subject-matter knowledge. It is true that schools teach students to learn content and knowledge. They teach students to read and do math. They also teach them history and physics. But ultimately what schools do is more than the learning or memorization of subject knowledge. Formal education serves multiple purposes (Labaree, 1997). Among them is the development of our youth as citizens, and the skills, values, and capacities of citizens are not only the memorization of the political systems in a society that can be taught in a class but also actual experiences with society and other members of society. Schools are in many ways a place for youth to experience society and learn how to interact with others in a civil and law-abiding way. Teachers or prepared adults are, therefore, needed to be the facilitator and organizer of such experiences.

Teachers cannot be replaced but their roles change with the introduction of technology (Zhao, 2018a; Zhao et al., 2015). One of the better ways to think about the relationship between teachers and technology is "never send a human to do a machine's job," a line we borrow from the movie *The Matrix*. The idea is not about technology replacing teachers. Rather it is about technology replacing and assisting certain functions that teachers traditionally perform.

Educational Uses of Technology

So what can technology do and teachers should not do?

Technology is invented to replace or facilitate human abilities. Automobiles, for example, were invented to replace the human ability to walk or run so we can move faster. Telephones were invented to boost the ability to send voices over farther distances. Robotics was invented to perform many functions that humans do not want to or are unable to perform as effectively and efficiently, or when there are great psychological and physical dangers. But almost no specific technology was invented for education. As a result, technology invented for other purposes has been adopted and adapted to fit the context of education. Thus, educational uses of technology are an interpretive process in which educators use technology to meet their needs.

This process of adoption and adaptation is largely influenced by the educational philosophies of educators. When a new technology is invented and brought to schools, educators typically make a number of judgments according to their views on education. First, they look at the technological functions and decide if they overlap with the functions they typically perform. If there are overlaps, they judge if the technology can make their work less demanding or more effective. If so, they may choose to use the technology to replace that aspect of their jobs. This is why PowerPoint and similar presentation technologies have been popular in schools.

Second, teachers look at the new technology and decide if it gives them new capabilities. That is, can the technology do something that they are unable to do? Educators have always been interested in making their teaching more interesting, more engaging, and more effective. But what they can do as humans can be limited. Technology can bring new possibilities. The internet, for example, makes it possible for students to interact with students from other schools in other countries. Thus, some educators, who are interested in promoting global collaboration and global competency, have been using the internet to engage students in global learning activities.

Third, educators also make a judgment about cost-effectiveness. That is, they need to be certain that the effectiveness of using the technology outweighs the cost (time, money, and potential negative outcomes) of learning to use the technology or having students use the technology. For instance, while smart devices can be used for learning in the classroom, some teachers or schools have decided to ban their uses in the classroom because they think they may distract the students from listening to the teacher. Virtual reality (VR) can also have educational benefits but is not widely used because it is still too costly.

Different educators have different educational philosophies. There has always been a battle between child-centered inquiry-based learning and content-centered direct instruction (Zhao, 2018c). The differences in philosophy lead educators to different judgments about technology, but they follow a similar interpretive process of using technology. It is important to note that the process is interpretive, subject to individual educator's perceptions, instead of objective and based on actual knowledge of the technology.

In this book, we are focusing on educating children for a complex and uncertain future. We are discussing developing children into rational, critical, and civil debaters and thinkers. We want our children to be social and emotionally healthy, to be curious and creative, and to be capable of discerning lies and untruths from facts and truth. We also want our children to care about their local communities, their nations, and the globe. We have an educational philosophy that can support an education for these purposes. We now use our philosophy to make a judgment about technological uses in education.

Access to the Global Resources

To paraphrase Seymour Papert, we can't teach people everything they need to know. The best we can do is to position them to find what they want to know when they are ready to learn it. One of the primary functions of today's technology is its capability to allow students and teachers to have access to educational resources globally. No matter where they are on earth, the internet has made it possible for them to gain access to educational resources created and put online by anyone anywhere on the planet. These resources can be courses and course materials such as massive open online courses on Coursera or edX, courses on Khan Academy, courses on YouTube, or online courses offered by education institutions. They can be websites of museums, art galleries, and libraries. They can be newspapers, books, journals, and magazines published online. They can also be video and audio recordings of performances, newscasts, movies, and TV programs.

There is no way to estimate how many resources are there, but it is definitely much more than any individual teacher can create. And new content is created and added to the global mass all the time. Moreover, these resources come in a diversity of formats including video, audio, text, or a combination of all. They are also of a multitude of styles and lengths.

Having access to global resources dramatically changes the role of the teacher. Students can now directly access online courses and other learning materials. They can watch the lessons, read the materials, and listen to the content. Teachers no longer need to be the only person in the classroom who knows the content and knows how to teach the content. In many ways, teachers no longer need to teach the content to the students. They need to organize materials for students. They may also need to organize students into smaller learning communities. They can also lead discussions and facilitate projects undertaken by students. But it is important to recognize that instructing content is no longer the teacher's primary job.

Access to Global Communities and Individuals

Another major capacity of today's technology is to enable access to people globally. Besides resources, today's students can also contact their peers, teachers, and experts located in other places. They can have video and audio conversations with people around the globe. They can also join global communities with synchronous and asynchronous communications. Of course, they can establish their own communities and invite people from other places to join.

No teacher can do this without technology. Thus, like access to global resources, access to global communities and individuals is what technology can do but individual teachers cannot do. This is a very powerful capacity that has significant implications for education in the Age of Globalization. First, teachers can and should collaborate with teachers in other countries so that their students can work together on common projects (Davis & Lindsay, 2012). For example, teachers in the United States can work with teachers in Russia and China on projects related to climate change and environmental protection. Second, teachers can have students conduct research globally by interviewing people in other places. For instance, a teacher in Australia interested in having his or her students understand the global impact of Covid-19 can have his or her students conduct interviews with people globally. Third, teachers can also have their students seek advice and help from others. The Human Interdependent Project (HIP), for example, recruits and trains students from different countries to support the learning of others. Native English-speaking students in the United States and Australia, for example, can provide tutoring to English learners in China.

Engage in Deep Learning

Technology has the potential to engage students in deep learning. Over the past few decades, researchers and innovators in education and technology have tried to use technology to assist teaching and learning. They have come up with a wide variety of ways to help students learn more deeply and more effectively with technology. They have tried teaching math and science through data visualization, allowing students to visualize abstract numbers and concepts (Mahmoudi et al., 2017; Presmeg, 2006). They have created software to enable students to plan and design experiments (Papert, 1993a, 1993b). They have experimented with situating students in simulated contexts to engage them in deep reasoning and decision-making (Ferguson et al., 2020).

There are also new developments in technology that provide exciting possibilities. For example, virtual reality and augmented reality (AR) technologies have been piloted in education for a long time, but recently they have become more accessible. VR and AR technologies give students immersive environments for them to experience and explore (Martín-Gutiérrez et al., 2017). They can bring faraway places such as museums, space stations, and the Arctic to the students, and the students can carefully manipulate, examine, and study them.

These technological capacities to engage students in deep learning, in experiencing new forms of learning, cannot be replicated by human teachers, no matter how good the teachers are. And there is no reason for teachers to compete with technology in these areas. Instead, teachers should make use of technology or allow students to use technology to learn.

Large-Scale Learning Environments

Technology has also made it possible to organize large learning environments for learners from around the world. These environments are globally distributed, large scale, and open to anyone wishing to join in. They include MOOCs (Bonk et al., 2015), fanfiction sites (Aragon et al., 2019), learning and play gaming communities such as Minecraft (Dezuanni, 2020) and Scratch (Resnick, 2017). Much of the learning in these environments is peer tutoring. Members of these communities typically have a strong interest in the subject and have different levels of expertise. They welcome and provide tutoring to newcomers. The learning in these environments can be extremely engaging and fruitful. And the learning is much more than simply the subjects but also about living and interacting with people from different cultural backgrounds online.

Teachers again do not have the capacity to create large-scale environments for their students, but they can do a number of things. First, they need to legitimize these environments as educational. It is easy for teachers and possibly parents to think of Minecraft or Scratch as play, joining a fanfiction site as a waste of time, or attending a MOOC as irrelevant to school work because it seems these sites are not directly part of the school curriculum. But research has shown their benefits and found them to be very valuable for cognitive and social development (Aragon et al., 2019; Dezuanni, 2020; Resnick, 2017). Thus, teachers and parents should at least accept that these activities could be valuable and meaningful for students. The second thing teachers can do is actively engage students in these learning environments. They could be part of a course, if appropriate, or an extracurricular activity. The third thing teachers could do is to support students participating in learning in these large-scale environments. These are authentic learning environments and there is no control over participants. So harmful things can happen and teachers can be of great value in helping students navigate these environments.

In summary, many technological capacities can be used in education. Human teachers do not have these capacities. Thus, we need to rethink the role of technology in relation to human teachers. Following the idea of "never send a human to do a machine's job," we can think about the classroom or the school as a learning ecosystem, in which teachers, technologies, textbooks, and other instructional materials are species interacting with students. To provide students with powerful learning experiences, teachers need not dominate the ecosystem all the time. Instead, they should allow technology and other materials to play their roles directly with students.

Blended learning, flipped classroom, hybrid learning, and online-merge-offline (OMO) classrooms are some of the keywords that have been created for different ways to use technology in education in recent years (Bonk & Graham, 2006; Means et al., 2013; Tucker, 2020). These keywords highlight the idea of allowing technology to do what it is best at and enabling teachers to let go of aspects of their job that can be done better by technology. They are all about combining the teacher and technology to deliver the best education for students.

Misuses

Technology can be and has been misused in education. Just because technology can do certain things does not mean that we should use it. Big data, for example, can sound very beneficial, but actually causes educational harm. Technology is very good at storing and spitting out data based on some algorithms. Schools have been asked to collect student data, all sorts of data that cover students' private information as well as their academic performances. These data can be analyzed and used for different purposes. One such use is called the early detection and prevention of dropouts. A piece of software was developed for this purpose and feeds school leaders and teachers suggestions about which student may drop out based on student and neighborhood data. While it sounds like a great idea, it is ethically wrong, and it can be completely wrong because the data and algorithm can be wrong as well. More important, while patterns may work for some students or even most students, they never capture all students. If a decision is made about one student, how does one know this student fits the pattern developed based on the data?

Another example of the misuse of big data technology recently took place in China, where a school brought in technology to monitor students' attention in class. The technology is worn on students' heads and watches students' eye movements. There are also video cameras in the classroom that watch the students' body movements and postures in class. The data are fed to a computer system that analyzes students' eye movements, body movements, and postures. The system then identifies students as paying attention or not. Again, it appears like a great use of technology because teachers and school leaders can now monitor students' attention and behavior at any time and can make educational adjustments when needed. The system can also give parents data about their children's actions in school. And, of course, schools can also make decisions to punish or reward students based on the system. However, this is an absolute misuse of technology. First, the accuracy of the data is questionable. Can a system truly measure students' attention based on eye movements and body postures? What if the algorithm and the observations are wrong or inaccurate? Second, assuming the system is accurate, should students be paying attention to the teacher all the time? Should all students be paying attention all the time? Third, does it really matter that much to watch students all the time and make decisions to correct their behaviors whenever possible? It is important to understand that learning is not necessarily paying attention to the teacher all the time. Perhaps being distracted or being deep in some thoughts is as important, if not more. Finally, what psychological pressure does the system put on students? How do people feel when watched all the time by a system and people behind the system?

Another possible misuse is an idea many education systems have espoused and have taken action to implement. The idea is simple. It is to have a system that keeps track of all students' performances and movements. Each student would have an ID in the system. No matter where the student goes, he or she can be tracked. Again, it sounds like a great idea because we can now know how a student moves around, grows up, and learns what and how deep the learning is.

However, such systems can be extremely dangerous. Once in the system, students can never escape. That means, whatever data are put in the system about a student can last a lifetime. The data can be connected or ported to future systems concerning employment or insurance. Whatever "bad" things a child did at age 7 can influence his or her employment 20 years later. Moreover, the data can affect teachers' and schools' decisions about students in the future. In education, there is a widespread and strong belief that students develop and learn linearly. In other words, students' growth in the past can predict their future. With this view, a student's data at age 10 can predict his or her life at age 30. However, human beings are not mechanical devices following a linear growth model. Human beings can and do change. Systems that track students all the time do not allow for the possibilities of change, especially changes that may be surprising. In other words, systems that track students all the time can serve to define and constrain the students.

There are other misuses. For example, artificial intelligence (AI) has been used to create personalized learning systems. These systems can guide students along a path of learning based on the student's performance and large amounts of data, which include the performances of large numbers of students. The system can decide what test items to give to each student and also what content a student should learn. Again, the systems appear smart and thus are sometimes called intelligent tutoring systems and can indeed help students learn what is prescribed within them. However, these systems offer instruction in similar ways to programmed learning promoted by behaviorists at the beginning of the last century. It is not personalized learning in the sense that students take the lead and construct knowledge through experimentation (Zhao, 2016, 2018b).

There are many possible ways to be misled by technology and to use technology in the wrong ways in education. As educators, what we need to consider first and foremost is the long-term educational outcomes of all children instead of short-term instructional outcomes (Zhao, 2017, 2018c). We should also be concerned that we may be causing unforeseen damage to students and society when technology is used to achieve certain apparently interesting goals. Many issues in education are uncertain and technology changes fast. Therefore, what we need to do is not rush toward quick solutions provided by technology, but instead we should be focused on more thoughtful uses of technology.

Reimagine Education with Technology

Covid-19 has brought massive disruption to education for more than a year. We have seen the negative consequences on students such as expected learning losses (CREDO, 2020; Dorn et al., 2020; Hanushek & Woessmann, 2020; Kuhfeld & Tarasawa, 2020; Shafer, 2020); however, at the same time, there have also been innovations. Using technology to offer remote learning is one such innovation. Online learning pods that parents organize or choose to participate in are another (Calarco, 2020).

The long-term economic and societal impact of the pandemic is still unknown, although many are expecting an economic downturn and social unease in the next few years. It is predictable that many education systems will suffer from less investment. Education systems will also be affected by parents, students, and possibly staff who have experienced isolation and remote learning. Parents and students may have different views on schools and learning. Staff may have different perspectives. And even entire education systems may have to be rethought in light of the experiences during the pandemic.

This is a great time to reimagine education. Given the power of technology discussed in this chapter, what can education be in the future? Given the relationship between teachers and technology, what can we do to promote better learning? Here are some possibilities.

First, we can imagine individual students becoming self-organized. Individual students, located in different places in the world, could choose to study one subject. They could become organized and then hire a teacher online or join a class online. They may be a group just staying for one course or many courses. It is likely that in the future, students would not have one school that dominates all their time. Instead, the students' "school" has different parts. In some sense, such systems already exist in many societies. Students go to school for formal learning and then they attend after-school tutoring sessions face to face and/or online. The after-school sessions are offered by outside agencies. But the change we are imagining would split the school day. Students may stay home and choose to attend an online course with one group and another course with another group. Then, the student may choose to join a local group of children for sports and recreation.

Second, it is also possible for teachers to run their own schools online or physically. This is not a new idea and many teachers already offer tutoring sessions this way. But it is possible that teachers can do more. Schools could, for example, allow their students to take online courses or students could decide to take online courses instead of courses offered in school. Individual teachers' online or face-to-face courses could be counted toward the formal curriculum.

Third, schools could outsource courses to teachers located in different places. Teachers no longer need to be in the same location as students, making it possible for schools to hire teachers globally. Students from one or more schools could take a course together from individual teachers who offer the course online. This is not entirely new either. MOOCs and Khan Academy are good examples.

Fourth, it is also possible that large schools will no longer be necessary. If students can learn both online and face to face, the functions of schools can change. Schools will only need to offer programs that require students to be physically together. Such programs may have to do with sports, physical laboratories, social gatherings, and community-based activities. But these activities can be small and there is no need to have hundreds or thousands of students in the physical school all the time.

Fifth, if students become the owners of their own learning, they could be working with a number of teachers in a local school plus teachers online. Students do not have to follow the same curriculum or pathway. They do not have to attend the same courses either. Thus, local schools can work with individual students on certain parts of the curriculum, especially the common curriculum that teaches the common values and skills of a society. But for the personalized curriculum that enables students to become unique and great, schools can allow students to learn online or from other schools (Zhao, 2021).

There can be other possibilities. We want to encourage educators, students, and education leaders to take this time to reimagine the possibilities brought about by technology and Covid-19. We have been treating schools as the only place of education for a long time. We have also been treating school time as the only time for learning for a long time. But we have come to a point where rethinking education is possible. Such rethinking should be about better education, not about better schools.

Summary

Technology has great potential for improving education. It can also be misused to the detriment of teachers and students. Technology offers students and educators access to knowledge and learning communities globally. It also enables students to carry out their own research and learn deeply about virtually any given topic. As we have seen, technology affords students opportunities to learn within large-scale communities such as MOOCs taught by experts from around the world.

Technology also enables teachers to assume different roles as guides, advisors, and co-learners rather than primarily purveyors of information. All of these are roles that technology is unlikely to supplant. Technology can relieve teachers of the more routine, repetitive, and boring work in instruction. They can be the organizers of educational ecosystems to help develop personalized learning journeys for every student.

To a degree never before seen, students can use technology to help them self-organize and pursue their individual as well as collective interests. They can choose their own teachers from virtually anywhere in the world. Teachers can, if they like, organize their own schools online and create global learning communities for themselves. The need for massive school buildings could diminish as teachers and students can teach and learn anywhere.

Of course, technology can and has been misused in education. Data on students, their behaviors and activities, and their families can be collected without their knowledge and used commercially. Technology designed to track student progress imposes a "one-size-fits-all" expectation for learning. Technology is and will continue to be a threat to students' and educators' right to privacy. We will all need to be ever vigilant.

References

Aragon, C. R., Davis, K., & Fiesler, C. (2019). *Writers in the secret garden: Fanfiction, youth, and new forms of mentoring*. Cambridge, MA: The MIT Press.

Bonk, C. J., & Graham, C. R. (2006). *The handbook of blended learning: Global perspectives, local designs* (1st ed.). San Francisco, CA: Pfeiffer.

Bonk, C. J., Lee, M. M., Reeves, T. C., & Reynolds, T. H. (Eds.) (2015). *MOOCs and open education around the world*. New York: Routledge.

Bransford, J. D., Brown, A. L., & Cocking, R. R. (Eds.) (2000). *How people learn: Brain, mind, experience, and school*. Washington, DC: The National Academies Press.

Calarco, J. (2020, July 24). 'Pod'-style learning benefits affluent kids and exacerbates education inequality — But it does address 3 key issues. Here's how to solve those problems equitably. *Business Insider*. Retrieved from: www.businessinsider.com/pod-style-learning-unequal-addresses-key-issues-how-to-solve-2020-7.

Christensen, C. M., Horn, M. B., & Johnson., C. W. (2010). *Disrupting class, expanded edition: How disruptive innovation will change the way the world learns* (2nd ed.). New York: McGraw-Hill.

CREDO (2020). *CREDO at Stanford University presents estimates of learning loss in the 2019–2020 school year*. Stanford, CA: CREDO. Retrieved from: https://credo.stanford.edu/sites/g/files/sbiybj6481/f/press_release_learning_loss.pdf.

Cuban, L. (1986). *Teachers and machines: The classroom uses of technology since 1920*. New York: Teachers College Press.

Cuban, L. (2001). *Oversold and underused: Computers in schools 1980–2000*. Cambridge, MA: Harvard University Press.

Davis, V., & Lindsay, J. (2012). *Flattening classrooms, engaging minds: Move to global collaboration one step at a time*. New York: Pearson.

Dezuanni, M. (2020). *Peer pedagogies on digital platforms: Learning with Minecraft let's play videos*. Cambridge, MA: MIT Press.

Dintersmith, T. (2018). *What school could be: Insights and inspiration from teachers across America*. Princeton, NJ: Princeton University Press.

Dorn, E., Hancock, B., Sarakatsannis, J., & Viruleg, E. (2020, December 8). COVID-19 and learning loss—Disparities grow and students need help. *McKinsey*. Retrieved from: https://www.mckinsey.com/industries/public-and-social-sector/our-insights/covid-19-and-learning-loss-disparities-grow-and-students-need-help

The European Parliament & The Council of the European Union. (2006, Dec. 18). Recommendation of the European Parliament and the Council on key competencies for lifelong learning. *Official Journal of the European Union*. Retrieved from: https://eur-lex.europa.eu/legal-content/EN/TXT/PDF/?uri=CELEX:32006H0962.

Ferguson, J., Astbury, J., Willis, S., Silverthorne, J., & Schafheutle, E. (2020). Implementing, embedding and sustaining simulation-based education: What helps, what hinders. *Medical Education*, 54, 915–924.

Goldin, C., & Katz, L. F. (2008). *The race between education and technology*. Cambridge, MA: Harvard University Press.

Hanushek, E. A., & Woessmann, L. (2020, September). The economic impacts of learning losses. *OECD*. Retrieved from: http://hanushek.stanford.edu/sites/default/files/publications/The Economic Impacts of Learning Losses_final_v1.pdf.

Kuhfeld, M., & Tarasawa, B. (2020, April). The COVID-19 slide: What summer learning loss can tell us about the potential impact of school closures on student academic achievement. *NWEA*. Retrieved from: www.nwea.org/content/uploads/2020/05/Collaborative-Brief_Covid19-Slide-APR20.pdf.

Labaree, D. F. (1997). Public goods, private goods: The American struggle over educational goals. *American Educational Research Journal*, *34*(1), 39–81.

Mahmoudi, M. T., Mojtahedi, S., & Shams, S. (2017). AR-based value-added visualization of infographic for enhancing learning performance. *Computer Applications in Engineering Education*, *25*(6), 1038–1052.

Martín-Gutiérrez, J., Mora, C. E., Añorbe-Díaz, B., & González-Marrero, A. (2017). Virtual technologies trends in education. *EURASIA Journal of Mathematics, Science and Technology Education*, *13*(2), 469–486.

Means, B., Toyama, Y., Murphy, R., & Baki, M. (2013). The effectiveness of online and blended learning: A meta-analysis of the empirical literature. *Teachers College Record*, *115*(3), 1–47.

Mitra, S. (2012, February 3). The hole in the wall project and the power of self-organized learning. Retrieved from: www.edutopia.org/blog/self-organized-learning-sugata-mitra.

Mitra, S. (2019). *The school in the cloud: The emerging future of learning*. Thousand Oaks, CA: Corwin.

National Academies of Sciences, Engineering, & Medicine. (2018). *How people learn II: Learners, contexts, and cultures*. Washington, DC: The National Academies Press.

Papert, S. (1993a). *The children's machine: Rethinking school in the age of the computer*. New York: BasicBooks.

Papert, S. (1993b). *Mindstorms: Children, computers, and powerful ideas* (2nd ed.). New York: Basic Books.

Perelman, L. J. (1992). *School's out: Hyperlearning, the new technology, and the end of education*. New York: William Morrow and Company Inc.

Pink, D. H. (2006). *A whole new mind: Why right-brainers will rule the future*. New York: Riverhead.

Presmeg, N. (2006). Research on visualization in learning and teaching mathematics: Emergence from psychology. In *Handbook of research on the psychology of mathematics education* (pp. 205–235). Rotterdam: Brill Sense.

Resnick, M. (2017). *Lifelong kindergarten: Cultivating creativity through projects, passion, peers, and play*. Cambridge, MA: The MIT Press.

Shafer, S. (2020, August 19). Overcoming COVID-19 learning loss. *Education Week*. Retrieved from: www.edweek.org/ew/issues/reopening-schools/overcoming-covid-19-learning-loss.html.

The Associated Press. (1923, May 13). Edison predicts film will replace teacher, books. Retrieved from: https://virginiachronicle.com/cgi-bin/virginia?a=d&d=HR19230518.2.11&e=-------en-20--1--txt-txIN-------

Tucker, C. R. (2020). *Balance with blended learning: Partner with your students to reimagine learning and reclaim your life*. Thousand Oaks, CA: Corwin.

Tyack, D., & Tobin, W. (1994). The "Grammar" of schooling: Why has it been so hard to change? *American Educational Research Journal, 31*(3), 453–479.

UNICEF. (2020, August 24). What will a return to school during the COVID-19 pandemic look like? *UNICEF*. Retrieved from: www.unicef.org/coronavirus/what-will-return-school-during-covid-19-pandemic-look.

Wagner, T. (2008). *The global achievement gap: Why even our best schools don't teach the new survival skills our children need – And what we can do about it*. New York: Basic Books.

Wagner, T. (2012). *Creating innovators: The making of young people who will change the world*. New York: Scribner.

Zhao, Y. (2012). *World class learners: Educating creative and entrepreneurial students*. Thousand Oaks, CA: Corwin.

Zhao, Y. (2016). *The take-action guide to world class learners. Book 1: How to make personalization and student autonomy happen*. Thousand Oaks, CA: Corwin, a SAGE company.

Zhao, Y. (2017). What works can hurt: Side effects in education. *Journal of Educational Change, 18*(1), 1–19.

Zhao, Y. (2018a). The changing context of teaching and implications for teacher education. *Peabody Journal of Education, 93*(3), 295–308.

Zhao, Y. (2018b). *Reach for greatness: Personalizable education for all children*. Thousand Oaks, CA: Corwin.

Zhao, Y. (2018c). *What works may hurt: Side effects in education*. New York: Teachers College Press.

Zhao, Y. (2020). Speak a different language: Reimagine the grammar of schooling. *International Studies in Educational Administration, 48*(1), 4–10.

Zhao, Y. (2021). *Learners without borders*. Thousand Oaks, CA: Corwin.

Zhao, Y., Zhang, G., Lei, J., & Qiu, W. (2015). *Never send a human to do a machine's job: Correcting the Top 5 mistakes in Ed Tech*. Thousand Oaks, CA: Corwin.

7
Where to from Here

As others have also noted, we are at a critical moment in history. Technology is advancing at an unprecedented pace. The world faces collective perils such as climate change and growing income inequalities. Yet the future remains to be written. The potential for a brighter future with widespread peace and prosperity is possible. At the same time, the potential for widening the income gap, escalating political divisions, increasing tribalism and geopolitical conflicts, and mounting climate catastrophes is also imaginable.

In many ways, we are facing these threats, in part, because in the race between education and technology, education is losing ground (Goldin & Katz, 2008). As technology has advanced over the last few decades, education has failed to keep pace. As technology has become more sophisticated, replaced more workers, and disrupted society and the economy, education has changed relatively little. Curriculum content, the structure of schools, and opportunities to learn, initially based on a 19th-century Prussian model, have changed incrementally.

As a result, a large proportion of the population is ill-equipped to fill the proliferating jobs in technology and take advantage of technological advances to improve their lives and their communities. Many are disenfranchised and disappointed, often resentful of the minority that have grown more prosperous. This minority have leveraged their wealth, expertise, and social and political connections to take advantage of these technological advances and transform the world, tightening their grip on power in the process. During the current pandemic

DOI: 10.4324/9781315682884-8

when so many have lost their jobs, a small minority have not only prospered but also augmented their wealth and power (Lane, 2021).

For the world to be a better place for all, much more radical change is needed. The Covid-19 pandemic reminds us of the misery to which the world is vulnerable. Virtually all economies in the world have experienced negative growth. Millions around the globe are unemployed. Billions of students and teachers have suffered major disruptions. In-school learning is another casualty of Covid-19. Even as the pandemic has accelerated the development, adoption, and use of some technologies, it has exacerbated economic and political divisions.

The full impact of the pandemic has yet to be realized. If the future was uncertain before the pandemic, it is dramatically more so now. Fortunately, vaccines are available to slow and, hopefully, stop the spread of the virus. The increased uncertainty and disruption it has generated, however, will be with us well into the future.

The Challenges Education Faces

At this critical moment, while there are many pressing issues and needs that policymakers and businesses must manage, the long-term challenges for education are numerous and urgent. The question is whether or not education can change sufficiently to prepare citizens who are capable of co-existing productively with robotics, acting with a global mindset, creating new jobs and organizations, forming more harmonious relationships locally and globally, engaging in rational and civil political discourse, and participating constructively in society. These capabilities and others are essential for an uncertain and potentially calamitous future.

As we have argued, education systems do not change easily or swiftly. Little has changed fundamentally over the last 100 years or so (Tyack & Cuban, 1995). Despite many innovations, successful experiments, informative research, and courageous efforts, our schools appear resistant to major changes. Until the pandemic, technology had not significantly disrupted the "grammar of schooling." Perhaps the greatest disruption to education in history, the pandemic has moved classrooms online, yet much remains the same. Subjects are still taught separately, students are still grouped by age, the curriculum remains much the same, and teachers still make most decisions about the organization and pace of opportunity to learn.

Our contention is that major changes are imperative – not just tweaks to the status quo but the revolution that Sir Ken Robinson has urged. Yet, major changes in education are rare and slow-moving. The complex systems that characterize education are difficult to change. These systems include vested interests who view change as potential threats to their power and the existing social relations within the system. As a result, education systems are stuck in the status quo, countenancing occasional innovations as safety valves to release pent-up dissatisfaction. Thus, those who are part of education systems are likely to view what we are proposing with, at best skepticism and, at worst, hostility.

The rub is that major changes cannot happen without systemic action. Pressure to act often comes from large-scale social movements. Individual schools, school leaders, teachers, students, families, citizen groups, and other non-school actors can and have pressured the system. Decades of concerted and targeted action by civil rights groups forced school integration upon a resistant system (Branch, 1988; Franklin, 2021). As the modern civil rights movement demonstrated, large-scale social movements can change public opinion. This, in turn, pressures systems and institutions to pay attention and adjust accordingly.

Recently, the #MeToo and Black Lives Matter movements are prime examples. Both started as grassroots movements whose messages resonated broadly with society and led to closer public scrutiny of systemic violence and injustice. They exposed pervasive sexism, sexual assault, and racism in workplaces, the media, the justice system, institutions, and police departments. Eventually, these movements grew and became sufficiently powerful that businesses, the legal system, armed forces, the media, education institutions, and various other organizations and government authorities could no longer minimize or ignore the systemic and institutional nature of the problems.

In this last chapter of the book, we attempt to pull together our thoughts and make them as accessible as possible to our readers. As we wrote in the introduction, our goal is not to produce definitive solutions to complex issues but rather to stimulate a conversation about the education our students need for a highly uncertain future. We hope to encourage everyone to rethink education, to reflect on the education of our children and youth with a "beginner's mind." We invite everyone to engage in thoughtful conversations about our children's future and how we can best prepare for a future, however wrought with uncertainty and threats, that also holds promise and opportunity.

The changes we have proposed are in all areas of education: schools, curriculum, pedagogy, opportunities to learn, assessment, and policy-making. A key condition is a redistribution of power so that practicing educators have greater voice and flexibility in deciding how learning should be organized, orchestrated, and assessed. They know what needs to be done both collectively and individually.

School choice schemes have afforded families more power without a corresponding increase in the power of educators. The history of education is replete with examples of schools, students, and teachers who have initiated and implemented changes (Zhao et al., 2019). Yet, most of these changes, while productive, remain localized and have not led to the systemic overhaul that we believe the future demands. As an aside, a major affordance of social media is that it provides teachers with online professional communities in which they can openly share their ideas and innovations as well as their worries and frustrations. These communities have been of particular importance during the pandemic when many teachers searched desperately for help on how best to teach remotely. Platforms such as TeachersConnect (teachersconnect.com), ProTeacher (proteacher.net), and Reddit subgroups enable teachers to find peers who are dealing with the same challenges they are facing.

Big Changes in What to Learn

Herbert Spencer's (Spencer, 1911) criteria for what knowledge is of greatest value still seem relevant. Spencer posed these questions: Does it help self-preservation? Does it help promote society? Does it inform parenting? Does it improve leisure time activities? Those in charge of education systems have asked similar questions in deciding what is to be taught. These authorities must decide what knowledge, skills, and dispositions students need now and in the future to improve society and the economy and to live full, satisfying, and productive lives.

A century or more ago, these decisions were easier to make. Many societies were mostly homogeneous and slow to change. Technology evolved much more slowly. As we have argued in Chapter 1, predicting the future was less challenging. Unless interrupted by disasters, life for most people closely resembled that of the previous generation. This relative predictability also made it easier to prescribe what students must learn. Economic sectors were fewer and changed at a modest pace. Fewer types of jobs were available and many required similar skills. Furthermore, the possibilities for individuals to create jobs for themselves were also limited.

This has changed radically at an accelerating pace. As we have discussed, technology has transformed the contexts and conditions in which our schools were initially founded. Predicting the jobs that will exist in 20 or 30 years is nigh on impossible. Technology transforms extant jobs, supplants workers, and eliminates whole industries even as it generates new jobs and industries. As automation and artificial intelligence (AI) technologies replace workers or make some jobs obsolete, innovators have demonstrated the capacity to create new jobs, many of which require humans not just machines. The growth of the gig economy, globalization, and online platforms has also produced new jobs. New technologies and the accompanying changes in our behaviors and relationships create opportunities for people to craft their own jobs to a degree never before seen or even imagined.

This is the context that demands we rethink education, especially the opportunities students have to learn and the character and content of these opportunities. We need to rethink the skills, knowledge, and dispositions that schools have traditionally offered. This is not to say that schools must discard existing curricula entirely. As we have argued, however, we need to rethink the standard fare and identify what is most essential for students who will be required to continue learning across their lifetimes. We are aware that educational history is littered with the remains of ideas better than ours on changing the school curricula and pedagogy (Hill & Celio, 1998; McDonald, 2014: Norris, 2004; Tyack & Cuban, 1997). Yet, in a world in which they will likely change jobs at least four, five, or more times in their lives, students' capacity to identify and learn what they need to know and be able to do is at least as important, if not more so, than the knowledge and skills represented in the traditional curriculum.

The necessary levels of research skills, resourcefulness, and mental acumen require students to develop unprecedented degrees of self-awareness. Self-awareness and self-monitoring prompt students to ask: What do I know? How reliable is what I think I know? What else do I need to learn? Where will I learn it? How will I know if my knowledge is sufficient? Fostering requisite levels of reflection, self-awareness, and skepticism have not typically been featured in the school curriculum or even regarded as the school's responsibility. Some teachers assume, on their own, the responsibility to teach these metacognitive skills and dispositions. They are, however, rarely included in curriculum standards or standardized assessments.

Such skills and dispositions have recently begun to appear in the various 21st-century skills recommendations we reviewed in Chapter 6 (Duckworth & Yeager, 2015). Most significant, however, is that school curricula have not traditionally targeted, taught, or tested these skills and dispositions. How to incorporate them into the conventional one-size-fits-all curriculum that is already overstretched is a major challenge, as we have noted.

Rethinking Curriculum and Opportunities to Learn

This is why a fundamental rethink of the curriculum is necessary. Governments are highly unlikely, however, to relinquish their monopoly on what citizens should know and be able to do. Schools have long been expected to acculturate students with a common body of knowledge, skills, and expected civic duties. If we have learned nothing else from nearly two centuries of government control of schools it is that mandated curricula do not ensure that students will have the opportunities they need to reach their full potential. Some scholars have argued that this is not even the primary function of schools. Bowles and Gintis (1976) posited that schools function primarily for social reproduction in capitalist societies. Greer (1972) similarly contended that the primary function of American schools is to maintain the status quo, thereby perpetuating the marginalization of the urban poor.

After the cancellation of the innovative and successful Renaissance program he and other teachers created, risk-taking teacher David Doneval concluded that high school is less an engagement in intellectual activities and more a rite of passage to adulthood akin to the Aboriginal Walkabout (Doneval, 1986).

Whatever your view of the function of schools, governments will continue to dictate curriculum content. Growing interest in 21st-century skills, dissatisfaction with assessment results, and the emergence of online resources, however, have combined to create an opening for new content and learning opportunities. In particular, interest has grown in the potential for personalized learning plans and opportunities among policymakers as well as educators, students, and families.

In 2012, the Race-to-the-Top legislation included the development of personalized learning environments as a "top priority" (Sykes et al., 2014). Some states and large urban districts have been working to institute more personalized experiences especially for high school students (Netcoh, 2017). Research evidence on the effects of personalized learning is consistently positive and shows that students in schools that have implemented personalized learning approaches outperform students in conventional schools (Pane et al., 2015).

Although the personalized approach has been primarily applied to learning the content in the mandated curriculum, it opens the door to even greater personalization. We can imagine a personalized curriculum built on each student's strengths and designed to support and guide the development of the student's interests and talents. This could be in addition to the mandatory curriculum, or some of the required curriculum could be part of the personalized learning experience. Personalization allows for the inclusion of skills and dispositions that are not subject specific such as creativity, collaboration, communication, critical thinking, self-direction, self-awareness, and self-regulation.

Personalization would allow for creating experiences designed to help students develop non-cognitive skills. These experiences would help students both realize their potential and better equip them to be contributing members of their communities and societies.

A key to students' psychological and social development is their sense of identity. Personalization creates opportunities for students to explore their identities. Shaping their identities are the communities of which they are a part. This prompted us to advocate for including local knowledge, values, and history in any curriculum (Zhao, 2021). To make room for all of this in the time frame of schools requires revisiting subject-matter curricula with the goal to identify the facts, information, concepts, algorithms, and methods in each traditional subject matter that constitute a foundation for subsequent learning. This is predicated on ensuring that students learn how to find resources and opportunities needed to pursue future learning in those subjects of greatest relevance and value to them.

This suggests that, in addition to the officially mandated curriculum (in its "essentials-only" form), each student needs a personalized curriculum. Students should have the opportunity to develop their strengths in their own way, capitalizing on a variety of resources that include educators and other experts. As we have discussed previously, a system that requires students to compete against each other in their mastery of a common set of skills and knowledge no longer serves students well. Except for the most basic knowledge and skills, forcing students to pursue the same educational outcomes seems unlikely to result in students reaching their full potential.

Personalized educational journeys seem likely to help students develop their strengths and interests into a unique "jagged profile" of abilities and interests. These unique profiles of abilities allow students to solve problems through creative and entrepreneurial capacities. In solving problems, students translate their unique abilities into something valuable as well as continue their learning. In this way, students can create their own jobs as business entrepreneurs, social entrepreneurs, policy and political entrepreneurs, or intrapreneurs (Zhao, 2012).

Rethinking Where to Learn

For most students, schools have been the primary, if not the only, place for formal learning. Even though technology has made it possible for students to learn online from outside-of-school resources, formal learning has continued to be largely the province of schools. Although the pandemic has forced schools to offer remote learning,

learning has remained under the control and direction of the schools and their educators.

Over time, instruction is delivered to groups of students organized by age. A group of 20, 30, or 60 students congregate in one room and sit behind their desks. They face an adult teacher, who stands in front of them and teaches all the students. To some degree, the learning place is technically the classroom with the school campus for other non-academic activities.

This arrangement made sense for several reasons. Teachers have long been viewed as the curators of knowledge. Following this belief, the transmission of knowledge happens only in their presence. Secondly, parents needed a safe place to send their children when they went to work. In addition, schools were where students learned to socialize with their peers. Finally, organizing students into groups made efficient use of the educator's time.

This long-standing practice makes much less sense today. As our experience during the pandemic has shown, technology enables learning virtually anywhere. In addition, whereas in the past, most of the physical resources available only in schools – textbooks, library books, curricular material, audio and video sources, and so on – are readily available online in digital form. In fact, learning resources have expanded way beyond what schools have offered. In addition to online modules, courses, books, journals, and so on, experts in all sorts of domains have become globally accessible.

Freed from the limitations posed by schools, any student can, in theory, now pursue his or her interests. A student interested in penguins can connect with an Antarctic wildlife specialist. A student of the French horn can book a lesson with a horn master. A student intrigued by electric vehicles can talk with an automotive engineer. A student who wants to start a non-profit for abandoned pets can converse with the chief executive officers (CEOs) of successful non-profits. The possibilities for personalized learning are virtually endless.

No longer limited to just the educators and peers in their school, students can reach out to educators and peers globally. Some schools have already established partnerships with schools in other countries through organizations such as the Global School Networks (globals choolnetworks.com).

Partnerships such as this offer opportunities for students to experience collaborating with peers from different backgrounds, cultures, and social classes. Digital simultaneous translation tools make language differences less of a barrier than they might previously have been. Years of research suggest that personal interactions between students from different races, ethnicities, and cultures reduce prejudice (Dovidio et al., 2021). In a sense, the new classroom is the globe, teachers are the guides, and students, individually or in virtual groups, are the investigators and problem-solvers.

Impeding this rethinking is culturally embedded ideas about what is genuine knowledge, who has it, and where it can be learned. As the pandemic has forced many families, educators, and policymakers to rethink their beliefs about knowledge, a return to the status quo ante seems unlikely. Whether deep rethinking required us to capitalize on technologies that challenge the notion that conventional classrooms are the most legitimate venue for learning remains to be seen.

As we have argued, many people have a stake in the status quo. Teachers' identity as teachers is, for many, tied to their classrooms and the accompanying sense of both responsibility and control. Understandably, they may be reluctant to turn over some of this responsibility and control to others. As we discuss below, allowing students to use online resources to pursue their learning needs and interests entails a change in teachers' roles.

Families may also be resistant to the prospects of their students relying heavily on online resources for learning. Just as the internet is a treasure trove of courses, information, data, and ideas, it also hosts sources that espouse potentially dangerous ideas and beliefs and flood searches with links to misinformation and conspiracy theories.

Government authorities may also have reservations about allowing sources they do not control to provide learning opportunities and information. School authorities already mandate various methods to limit student access to certain sources of information and ideas. As schools move to expand personalized learning that typically relies, in part, on internet resources, we can envision ever-tighter controls over access to such resources. This would, of course, undermine one of the most promising affordances of digital sources.

Rethinking How to Learn

Mere information gathering, memorization, and answering already-answered questions are not the modes of learning that will best serve students in the future. As the various lists of 21st-century skills emphasize, future jobs and social and environmental challenges will require citizens who think analytically and critically, collaborate to creatively solve unpredictable problems, and approach new information and ideas skeptically. To develop these capacities requires, in the present, opportunities to learn that differ significantly from those to be observed in most classrooms.

The movement toward project-based learning that focuses on solving real-world problems is a step in this direction. The process starts with students collectively considering various societal and environmental problems. A critical step, this evaluation includes consideration of the relative urgency of various problems, the availability and accessibility of resources, and the group's capacity to address the problems. Once a problem is identified, all group members are engaged in developing a solution. If circumstances permit, the group might be involved in implementing the solution or reporting to those responsible for addressing it. Finally, inviting "critical friends" to evaluate the solution generates feedback to help the group improve the process (Zhao, 2012, 2018b).

A problem-oriented learning approach changes the orientation of learning. Rather than information, procedures, and ideas whose application is at best obscure, learning is clearly linked to identifying and solving specific, authentic problems. Identifying problems and devising solutions help students to develop the entrepreneurial and creative mindset that prepares them to create innovative tools, services, art, and organizations. These are essential to a brighter future not only for students but also for the societies in which they will be living.

Learning in collaborative groups also takes advantage of the social nature of learning. As psychologists have discovered over the past century, although learning may ultimately unfold intra-personally, it is mediated by our sociocultural contexts (Brown & Duguid, 2000; Luria, 1976; Wertsch et al., 1995). As students learn with and from one another, their understandings of themselves as learners change. Such metacognition is essential to their development as lifelong learners. With proper guidance, such social learning can also help them learn to take the perspective of others – a disposition identified in various 21st-century skills recommendations.

Big Changes in the Role of the Learner

The rethinking of the learning process implies a rethinking of the learner's role. No longer a more or less passive receptor of information, learners become active agents and managers of their learning. Many if not all students begin school as active learners. This is one of evolution's gifts. Were we not born learners and creators, our species would have died out on the African savannah millennials ago. As they progress through preschool and kindergarten, students encounter the prescribed curriculum. Whatever their interests or abilities, they find themselves expected to learn a predetermined myriad of information, skills, rules, procedures, relational norms, and behaviors. The lucky ones have teachers who try to identify and cultivate their individual interests. Many, however, are not so lucky. Their interest in and curiosity about the world that is their birthright find the school culture and curriculum barren ground.

This need not be the case when technology affords multiple tools for students, even at early ages, to explore whatever sparks their interest and enthusiasm. With guidance from educators and others, they can become designers of their own educational pathways. In so doing, along the pathways are opportunities for them to continuously cultivate the self-regulating and self-monitoring skills and dispositions that characterize successful independent learners. Although maturation of these skills and dispositions requires time and practice, strategies exist to support the changes (Wehmeyer & Zhao, 2020).

Rethinking the Role of the Teacher

Problem-focused, personalized learning not only changes the role of learners but also that of teachers. Despite models of active learning that have been around for decades and promoted in teacher preparation programs, most teachers seem to prefer a conventional classroom role. It offers the comfort of familiarity and, in policy environments that discourage risk-taking, it is the safest route. To support the development of independent, collaborative, critical, and skeptical problem-solvers demands that teachers adopt different roles, primary of which are guides and question-askers.

These roles involve organizing students to identify problems and unanswered questions, guiding them in their discussions and debates, asking questions that provoke deep thinking and reflection, and helping them find trustworthy sources and evidence. In organizing collaborative work, the teacher's role would include ensuring the inclusion of diverse voices and working with students to establish group norms, procedures, and protocols for discussions. Monitoring group progress and being available as a consultant, mediator, or "critical friend" also fit into this role.

In a personalized learning environment in which students design their own curriculum, the role of the teacher is that of facilitator, adviser, and supporter (Zhao, 2018a). In this role, teachers help students identify the resources and materials they need to pursue their personalized curriculum. As they are pursuing skills and knowledge of their choosing, students have less need for teachers to serve as motivators, an aspect of teaching that many teachers find challenging, especially at the secondary-level learning journey. In poll after poll, a majority of high school students report being bored most of the time they are in class. Personalized learning is not a cure-all for teenage boredom but it holds the promise of reducing it significantly.

These roles do not diminish the importance of teachers. Rather, they accentuate the critical role they play in supporting individual students in reaching their potential. Technology can relieve teachers of the tedious, repetitive, and predictable aspects of teaching, affording them the time and energy to engage more fully with their students (Zhao et al., 2015). Their role as transmitters of knowledge is largely supplanted by a different role as cultivators of the talents, interests, character, values, and ethics of individual students. This is precisely the role to which many teachers aspire and some have already achieved.

Rethinking Schools

Because they are parts of complex systems, the foci of multiple interest, and perennial battlegrounds for culture wars, schools are difficult to change. Schools have become a language with their own grammar (Tyack & Tobin, 1994). As we have noted, school governance in highly decentralized systems like the United States is shared by local and state school boards, state departments of education, governors' offices, legislatures, and the federal government. Publishers, teachers' unions, the media, testing companies, foundations, parent and community organizations, think tanks, non-profits, civic organizations, political parties, higher education institutions, tech companies – the list of those who monitor and feel they have a stake in schools is seemingly endless. Adding to the complexity of the environment are the critical roles they play in many communities that extend well beyond education. In some communities, schools are also major employers, recreation and community centers, libraries, after-school care providers, meeting spaces, and health clinics.

Considering the complexity of both the governance and the environment of schools, we are left wondering whether significant change is possible. But we humans created schools as they are so we should be able to change them (Zhao, 2020a, 2020b, 2020c). From a historical perspective, modern schools are only about 200 years old whereas we have been living in communities since at least Neolithic times. If there were ever a time to rethink schools, the time is now.

Expecting change to come from within existing systems seems unrealistic. Expecting change to happen quickly seems similarly unrealistic. Expecting change to be widely and enthusiastically embraced is very unlikely, although those who have been poorly served by the existing systems may welcome it. Expecting change agents to emerge from the existing systems also seems unlikely but by no means impossible. More likely, as we have seen with changes in other spheres, change will be driven by groups and individuals who offer compelling ideas about education that enhance the life chances of all students, not just the fortunate ones.

Above we described the learning opportunities that support the intellectual, social, psychological, and ethical development of students. We also described the roles that teachers can play in this development. The question now is: How can we rethink schools so they support students and teachers in their new roles and better prepare students for an uncertain future?

As a start, existing schools can collaborate to create networked schools. The Global Online Academy (GOA),[1] for example, is an online school that provides courses for students who attend over 200 schools globally. The GOA started as a consortium of a small number of prestigious private schools and gradually expanded. Member schools pay fees to the GOA and their students can take the GOA courses together with students from other member schools. The courses are regarded the same as the courses taught in students' home schools. Teachers from member schools receive professional development to teach online and are encouraged to offer courses via the GOA.

Establishing the GOA is a remarkable achievement for the founding elite and prestigious schools. The fact that they allow their students to take courses from other schools and share their own staff with others globally is fairly new. If this model were to spread across the educational world, what would it mean? It would mean that schools anywhere could share resources and staff with each other, and that students could participate virtually with students from schools around the world. Teachers in any network school can teach students in any other network school in the world. Students have access to a variety of courses and teachers. International networks also create the potential for students to collaborate on projects with peers from other countries.

Another possibility has emerged from the catastrophic Covid-19 pandemic. Families, desperate to continue their children's education amid the chaos of schools opening and closing, devised "learning pods" (Calarco, 2020). Through various social media, groups of concerned parents connected and arranged to hire a teacher who would teach their children. The parents may not even live in the same school district much less send their children to the same schools. These arrangements that seem to typically accommodate eight or fewer students are similar to those that homeschooling families organize for their children. In the case of learning pods, the pods appear much more likely to be in relatively affluent areas where families have the means to support their share of a teacher's salary. A possibility is that some families may choose to continue supporting these pods even after schools fully reopen. Whether or not enough families would or could support enough of these arrangements to disrupt schools is not clear.

Yet a third possibility is that schools could evolve into a collection of learning communities either run in cooperation with teachers or even fully student managed. Such learning communities, organized around students' interests and needs, could network with other student learning communities locally, nationally, and globally. The central idea is that students take charge of creating and managing these communities.

Networked schools have shown promise in addressing inequities. Chu et al. (2021) studied the effects of the Gates Foundation–Funded Networks for School Improvement (NSI) and found that they showed "considerable potential to help schools and districts dismantle barriers to opportunity for marginalized students." Moreover, the most effective NSIs were those in which teachers used greater independence to strengthen their problem-solving approaches. Notably, Gates backed off from its prior strategy of dictating that project districts and schools adopt the foundation's prescribed approaches. Rather, the educators in the NSI schools were allowed to develop their own strategies and approaches.

Rethinking schools could also include school size. Micro-schools could offer better experiences for many educators, students, and families than the large comprehensive schools that have resulted from consolidation policies over the past 70 years. Smaller schools require less space and offer more personalized learning opportunities. In the 1960s and 1970s, storefront schools sprang up in cities across the country in communities that wished to offer their children more relevant and engaging learning opportunities than those available in the large local public schools (McLaughlin, 2014). Storefront schools also, figuratively, knocked down the walls and capitalized on the rich learning opportunities their cities offered. Local businesses, experts, and elders joined the storefront teachers thereby creating a faculty representing highly diverse knowledge and skills.

Renpro, as Doneval's program was called, represents yet another way of restructuring existing schools. The "school-within-a-school" (SWS) concept has been around since at least the 1950s when school leaders divided Newton High School in Newton, Massachusetts, into four "houses" (Lee & Ready, 2007). We know that all students but especially marginalized students and those in under-resourced schools benefit from higher levels of interaction with their teachers. Breaking down schools and classrooms into smaller groups appears to be an approach that fits with existing school systems. As the Gates' Small School project and the Renpro example demonstrate, however, system dynamics and prevailing school cultures and structures can undermine efforts to create smaller learning communities.

Rethinking Assessment

The well-worn adage that "teachers teach what is tested" is a primary motivation for rethinking assessment. It is no less true that evidence of the effects of instruction is essential as a basis for improving opportunities to learn. The question is: What forms of assessment will provide students, educators, and policymakers with the most trustworthy and actionable feedback to inform improvement?

We have many different forms of assessment for different purposes. To support the new curriculum content, learning opportunities, and learning community configurations requires rethinking all of our assessments. Perhaps most critically, we need to rethink large-scale standardized assessments whose primary effect seems to have been increasing the pressure on schools and educators, not improving student learning. These assessments include international assessments such as the Programme for International Student Assessment (PISA) and national or state accountability assessments. Assessments do provide data for essential research purposes. Their use as a means to judge the quality of teaching or student learning is not only far less useful, but it may also have negative consequences. The idea that students and educators be evaluated based on one body of knowledge and skills or on one type of assessment seems patently unfair and misleading. Unfair because the results lack context. We do not know the "dosage" students have received for any given item or sets of items. PISA, for instance, tests 15-year-olds around the world. But do all 15-year-olds receive the same level of instruction on the mathematical items that the psychometricians at the Organization for Economic Co-operation and Development (OECD) choose to include? Involving practicing educators in selecting the content to be tested seems a helpful step but those educators who are consulted represent a small, non-random sample of the teachers worldwide whose students are tested.

In addition, the data can be misleading as a country's general mathematics or reading scores obscure variability. When scores are broken down geographically, significant disparities emerge, school to school, district to district, region to region. Yet, policymakers tend to focus on the aggregate scores and the comparative rankings. Rather than rethinking policies, authorities are tempted to game the system. After China fell in the rankings on the 2012 PISA as a result of adding three other provinces to the original Shanghai-only sample, authorities substituted a higher-wealth province with a strong education system, Zhejiang, for a less-wealthy district with a weaker education system serving millions of migrant families, Guangdong. Voila! China resumed it place atop the PISA scorecard in 2015.

More trustworthy and informative data are provided by "authentic assessments." Such assessments are tied directly to the learning opportunities that students experience. Moreover, if appropriate for the content, authentic assessment measures students' ability to apply their learning to real-world problems. To authentically assess learning from collaborative problem-solving projects requires, from the outset, identification of the evidence of success as well as the criteria applied to the evidence. In this way, students can assess their own learning based on the outcomes of the project.

Authentic assessments are similarly valuable as students pursue their personalized learning plans. In developing their plans, students benefit from determining their own markers of success as well as benchmarkers that inform the students, teachers, and families of their progress along the way.

If students are to develop 21st-century skills, assessment programs need to capture the development of these recommended skills and dispositions as well as the conventional curriculum content. This is a challenge for educators. How do we best assess students' creativity, critical thinking, collaborative and communication skills as well as their self-awareness, ethics, and civic engagement? Conventional assessments seem like dull tools for such a job. On the 2018 PISA, the OECD experimented with online simulations to measure students' collaborative skills. Such an approach seems promising. The most trustworthy approach, however, might be to train teachers to use observational protocols designed to collect information on students' interactions and classroom behaviors. Early childhood educators have long been trained to observe and document the social skills and dispositions of their charges. Yet, although social and emotional learning (SEL) program evaluation tools exist, educators lack instruments necessary to gauge their success in helping students develop non-cognitive and social and emotional skills (Grant et al., 2017). Lacking credible tools for measuring the impact of their efforts to help students develop 21st-century skills and dispositions, most teachers will continue to focus on the knowledge and skills traditionally measured on standardized tests. What's tested will continue to be what's taught.

Summary

A sense of urgency motivated us to write this book. Our concern is that education systems have been slow to seize the opportunity created by the pandemic to rethink the how, where, when, and what of schooling. A future best characterized as uncertain and largely unpredictable requires knowledge, skills, and dispositions that have not found their way into most schools that remain in the grip of neoliberal policies that include accountability, high-stakes testing, marketization, and standardization. Organizations such as the OECD recognize that as current jobs disappear and new jobs appear in a rapidly evolving global economy and leisure time increases, people who thrive in this new world will need skills such as creativity, critical thinking, teamwork, inquiry, communication, logical and ethical reasoning, and mental and social flexibility. Although essential, these are not enough. Those who thrive in the future will also value diverse ideas and voices, are critical of new information and ideas, aware of their strengths and weaknesses, open to criticism and rethinking, and disposed to continuous learning and relearning.

Helping all students develop these skills and dispositions is a challenge and a different mission for education systems. Instilling knowledge of the traditional subject matters, work habits valued by businesses, and allegiance to their communities and the nation-state is a mission suited to an industrial world. The emerging new world would seem to require a rethinking of this mission. This is a world in which machines are replacing most humans in manual and routine jobs, many current enterprises are dying as unforeseen enterprises are appearing, organizations are growing flatter and decision-making more distributed and team based, collaboration and co-creation across national boundaries are increasingly the norm, technology-based opportunities for innovation and creativity abound, access to information (and misinformation) continues to grow, and information itself is expanding as AI enables us to extract new knowledge and insights.

As we have argued, to manage and capitalize on these dramatic changes require a rethinking of all aspects of education systems – curriculum, pedagogy, opportunities to learn, assessments, the roles of teachers and students, school organization and governance, and educational policies.

Also needed is a rethink of how to bring about these changes. Greater engagement of frontline educators, communities, and students is necessary but not sufficient. Innovations and changes are largely at the mercy of policymakers who control the flow of resources and who establish and maintain regulations. Outside groups can pressure policymakers to support or reject proposals for needed changes, and foundations and corporations can provide resources to challenge the government's grip on the education system.

We are mindful that none of what we are suggesting will be easy to pull off. If it were, many of the changes would have happened already. We are also mindful of Mencken's warning that for every complex problem, there are solutions that are clear, simple, and wrong. If, however, we are to profoundly rethink how well we are preparing our students for the future, we need to begin conversations that include all the actors in the system, anticipating that disagreement is inherent to the process. Provoking conversation that engages the various actors in and outside the system is the goal of this book.

We are in a very interesting and challenging time. This is a great time to make big changes. Changes can take place in what students should learn, how they should learn, and where learning should take place. Schools and teachers should also be making changes. And, of course, assessment needs changes as well. The big message is that schooling can no longer continue as it has been. Students have to be more in charge of their learning. And schools need a massive transformation.

Note

1 https://globalonlineacademy.org/

References

Bowles, S., & Gintis, H. (1976). *Schooling in capitalist America: Educational reform and the contradictions of economic life*. New York: Basic Books.

Brown, J., & Duguid, P. (2000). *The social life of information*. Cambridge, MA: Harvard Business Review Press.

Calarco, J. (2020, July 24). 'Pod'-style learning benefits affluent kids and exacerbates education inequality — But it does address 3 key issues. Here's how to solve those problems equitably. *Business Insider*. Retrieved from https://www.businessinsider.com/pod-style-learning-unequal-addresses-key-issues-how-to-solve-2020-7.

Chu, E., Kinlaw, A., & Snyder, M. (2021). Accelerating network-based change. Teachers College Record, Date Published: February 24, 2021. https://www.tcrecord.org. ID Number: 23612, Date Accessed: 2/28/2021 7:03:36 AM.

Doneval, D. (1986). *High school: American walk-about*. Occasional paper series, Vol. X, No. 2. Andover, MA: Regional Laboratory for Educational Improvement for the Northeast & Islands.

Dovidio, J, Schelhass, F., & Pearson, A. (2021). Prejudice. Oxford research encyclopedia. Retrieved from: https://oxfordre.com/psychology/psychology/view/10.1093/acrefore/9780190236557.001.0001/acrefore-9780190236557-e-263.

Duckworth, A. L., & Yeager, D. S. (2015). Measurement matters: Assessing personal qualities other than cognitive ability for educational purposes. *Educational Researcher*, *44*(4), 237–251.

Goldin, C., & Katz, L. F. (2008). *The race between education and technology*. Cambridge, MA: Harvard University Press.

Grant, S., Hamilton, L., Wrabel, S., Gomez, C., Auger, A., Whitaker, A., Tamargo, J., Unlu, F., Chavez-Herrerias, E., Baker, G., Barrett, M., & Harris, M. (2017). S*ocial and emotional learning interventions under the every student succeeds act*: *Evidence review*. Santa Monica, CA: RAND.

Greer, C. (1972). *The great school legend: A revisionist iInterpretation of American public education*. New York: Basic Books, Inc.

Hill, P., & Celio, E. (1998). *Fixing urban schools*. Washington, DC: Brookings Institution Press.

Lane, C. (2021, January 24). The rich got richer during the pandemic. We need to claw back their gains. *The Washington Post*. Retrieved from: https://www.washingtonpost.com/opinions/the-rich-got-richer-during-the-pandemic-we-need-to-claw-back-their-gains/2021/01/25/d17c8a44-5f32-11eb-9430-e7c77b5b0297_story.html.

Lee, V., & Ready, D. D. (2007). *Schools within schools: Possibilities and pitfalls of high school reform*. New York: Teachers College Press.
Luria, A. (1976). *Cognitive development: Its cultural and social foundations*. Cambridge, MA: Harvard University Press.
McDonald, J. (2014). *American school reform*. Chicago, IL: University of Chicago Press.
McLaughlin, M. (2014). Storefront revolutionary: Martin Sostres Afro-Asian bookshop, black liberation culture, and the new left, 1964–75. *The Sixties*, *7*(1), 1–27. doi: 10.1080/17541328.2014.930265.
Netcoh, S. (2017). Students' experiences with personalized learning: An examination using self-determination theory. Graduate College Dissertations and Theses. 738. https://scholarworks.uvm.edu/graddis/738.
Norris, D. (2004). *The promise and failure of progressive education* Lanham, MD: Scarecrow Press/Rowman & Littlefield.
Pane, J. F., Steiner, E. D., Baird, M. D., and Hamilton, L. S. (2015). *Continued progress: Promising evidence on personalized learning*. Santa Monica, CA: RAND Corporation, RR-1365-BMGF, as of February 26, 2021: https://www.rand.org/pubs/research_reports/RR1365.html.
Spencer, H. (1911). What knowledge is of most worth. In H. Spencer (Ed.) *Essays on education and kindred subjects*. London: Dent/Aldine Press.
Sykes, A., Decker, C., Verbrugge, M., & Ryan, K. (2014). *Personalized learning in progress: Case studies of four race to the top-district grantees' early implementation*. Washington, DC: District Reform Support Network.
Tyack, D., & Cuban, L. (1995). *Tinkering toward utopia: A century of public school reform*. Cambridge, MA: Harvard University Press.
Tyack, D., & Tobin, W. (1994). The "Grammar" of schooling: Why has it been so hard to change? *American Educational Research Journal*, *31*(3), 453–479.
Wehmeyer, M., & Zhao, Y. (2020). *Teaching students to become self-determined learners*. Alexandria, VA: ASCD.
Wertsch, J., del Rio, P., & Alverez, A., Eds. (1995). *Sociocultural studies of mind (learning in doing: Social, cognitive and computational perspectives)*. Cambridge University Press.
Zhao, Y. (2012). *World class learners: Educating creative and entrepreneurial students*. Thousand Oaks, CA: Corwin.
Zhao, Y. (2018a). The changing context of teaching and implications for teacher education. *Peabody Journal of Education*, *93*(3), 295–308.
Zhao, Y. (2018b). *Reach for greatness: Personalizable education for all children*. Thousand Oaks, CA: Corwin.
Zhao, Y. (2020a). COVID-19 as a catalyst for educational change. *Prospects*, *49*(1), 29–33. doi: 10.1007/s11125-020-09477-y.
Zhao, Y. (2020b). Speak a different language: Reimagine the grammar of schooling. *International Studies in Educational Administration*, *48*(1), 4–10.
Zhao, Y. (2020c). Tofu is not cheese: Rethinking education amid the COVID-19 pandemic. *ECNU Review of Education*, *3*(2), 189–203.

Zhao, Y. (In Press). *Learners without borders*. Thousand Oaks, CA: Corwin.
Zhao, Y., Emler, T. E., Snethen, A., & Yin, D. (2019). *An education crisis is a terrible thing to waste: How radical changes can spark student excitement and success*. New York: Teachers College Press.
Zhao, Y., Zhang, G., Lei, J., & Qiu, W. (2015). *Never send a human to do a machine's job: Correcting the Top 5 mistakes in Ed Tech*. Thousand Oaks, CA: Corwin.

Index

Made in United States
Orlando, FL
30 July 2022